Charles F. Richardson

A Primer of American literature

Charles F. Richardson

A Primer of American literature

ISBN/EAN: 9783743332164

Manufactured in Europe, USA, Canada, Australia, Japa

Cover: Foto ©ninafisch / pixelio.de

Manufactured and distributed by brebook publishing software (www.brebook.com)

Charles F. Richardson

A Primer of American literature

A PRIMER

OF

AMERICAN LITERATURE.

BY
CHARLES F. RICHARDSON.

BOSTON:
HOUGHTON, OSGOOD AND COMPANY.
The Riverside Press, Cambridge.
1878.

COPYRIGHT, 1878,
BY CHARLES F. RICHARDSON.

All rights reserved.

RIVERSIDE, CAMBRIDGE:
STEREOTYPED AND PRINTED BY
H. O. HOUGHTON AND COMPANY.

CONTENTS.

CHAPTER I.
1620–1775.

		PAGE
1.	THE BEGINNING	7
2.	THE THEOLOGICAL ERA	9
3.	INCREASE AND COTTON MATHER	10
4.	ELIOT'S INDIAN BIBLE	12
5.	ROGER WILLIAMS	13
6.	MINOR WRITERS OF THE SEVENTEENTH CENTURY	14
7.	YALE COLLEGE	15
8.	JONATHAN EDWARDS	16
9.	THE FOLLOWERS OF EDWARDS	18
10.	BENJAMIN FRANKLIN	18
11.	FRANKLIN AS A WRITER	20
12.	FRANKLIN AS A SCIENTIST AND DIPLOMATIST	21
13.	MINOR WRITERS OF THE EIGHTEENTH CENTURY	21

CHAPTER II.
1775–1812.

1.	THE REVOLUTIONARY PERIOD	23
2.	GEORGE WASHINGTON AS A WRITER	24
3.	THOMAS JEFFERSON	24
4.	THE FEDERALIST	25

		PAGE
5. Thomas Paine	. . . . . .	26
6. Poets	. . . . . .	27
7. The First Novelist	. . . . .	28
8. Historians and Other Writers	. . .	28

CHAPTER III.

1812–1861.

1. Theological Changes	. . . . .	30
2. William Ellery Channing	. . .	32
3. Other Theological Writers	. . .	34
4. The Knickerbocker School	. . .	38
5. Washington Irving	. . . .	38
6. James Kirke Paulding	. . . .	43
7. Joseph Rodman Drake	. . . .	44
8. Fitz-Greene Halleck	. . . .	45
9. Other Early Poets	. . . .	46
10. William Cullen Bryant	. . .	48
11. Henry Wadsworth Longfellow	. .	50
12. Longfellow's Poems	. . . .	52
13. Longfellow's Prose Works	. . .	54
14. Longfellow's Dante	. . . .	55
15. John Greenleaf Whittier	. . .	56
16. Holmes's Poems	. . . . .	58
17. Holmes's Prose Works	. . .	59
18. James Russell Lowell	. . . .	60
19. Edgar Allan Poe	. . . .	63
20. Other Poets	. . . . .	64
21. Orators	. . . . . .	66
22. Historians	. . . . .	66
23. Richard Hildreth	. . . .	67
24. George Bancroft	. . . .	67
25. John Gorham Palfrey	. . . .	68
26. William Hickling Prescott	. . .	69

CONTENTS.

		PAGE
27.	JOHN LOTHROP MOTLEY	69
28.	OTHER HISTORIANS	70
29.	TRAVELERS	71
30.	FICTION. — JAMES FENIMORE COOPER	72
31.	NATHANIEL HAWTHORNE	74
32.	OTHER NOVELISTS	77
33.	EMERSON AND THE CONCORD AUTHORS	80
34.	MISCELLANEOUS WRITERS	81
35.	SCIENTIFIC AND SPECIAL WRITERS	84

CHAPTER IV.

AFTER 1861.

1.	LITERATURE OF THE CIVIL WAR	85
2.	POETS	87
3.	BAYARD TAYLOR	88
4.	RICHARD HENRY STODDARD	89
5.	JOHN GODFREY SAXE	89
6.	JOHN TOWNSEND TROWBRIDGE	90
7.	WALT WHITMAN	90
8.	JOAQUIN MILLER	91
9.	FRANCIS BRET HARTE	92
10.	JOHN HAY	92
11.	THOMAS BAILEY ALDRICH	93
12.	EDMUND CLARENCE STEDMAN	95
13.	THE PIATTS	95
14.	OTHER POETS	96
15.	WILLIAM DEAN HOWELLS	98
16.	THEODORE WINTHROP	99
17.	EDWARD EGGLESTON	100
18.	JULIAN HAWTHORNE	100
19.	HENRY JAMES, JR.	101
20.	ELIZABETH STUART PHELPS	101
21.	LOUISA MAY ALCOTT	102

22. Harriet Prescott Spofford 103
23. Other Novelists 103
24. American Humor 104
25. Charles Dudley Warner 107
26. James Parton 108
27. Edward E. Hale 108
28. Thomas Wentworth Higginson . . . 109
29. Miscellaneous Writers 109

A PRIMER

OF

AMERICAN LITERATURE.

CHAPTER I.

1620–1775.

1. THE BEGINNING. — As soon as the English colonists landed on American shores, at Jamestown and Plymouth, they began to think of the establishment of schools of sound learning: in Virginia for the purpose of educating the Indians, and in Massachusetts Bay for the supply of church pastors. By 1619 the proposed Virginia university possessed, as gifts from English donors, fifteen thousand acres of land and fifteen hundred pounds in money, and its early establishment at Henrico, on the James River, was prevented only by a general Indian massacre on March 22, 1622, when three hundred and forty persons, including the superintendent of the university, lost their lives. Nothing further was done toward establishing a Virginia college until 1660, and the College of

William and Mary, the outcome of the original idea, did not receive its charter until 1693. The Puritans of Massachusetts were more fortunate and more prudent than the Cavaliers of Virginia, for they suffered no loss by any extensive massacre, and they depended upon themselves instead of looking for help from England, where, indeed, they had few friends. Their "school or college" at Newtown (Cambridge) was begun in 1636 with only four hundred pounds in money, but two years later it received a sum amounting, it is supposed, to seven or eight hundred pounds, together with a respectable library, by the will of John Harvard, the young Charlestown minister whose name Harvard University now bears. From that time its income was small but sure, and its existence during the latter part of the seventeenth century did much to give Massachusetts the literary start which the greater wealth and the imported instructors of the Virginia institution could not offset. In both colonies, however, schools, and their inevitable result, book-making, appeared with creditable promptness; and those colonists who first taught or wrote have their posthumous reward in the most vigorous offshoot that the literature of any nation has ever been able to put forth. American literature has a right to a share in the heritage of the countrymen of Cædmon and Chaucer and Shakespeare; but its enforced independence and its familiarity with new surroundings have given it character and deserts of its own.

THE THEOLOGICAL ERA. — At the outset American literature was imitative; the first writers were of English birth and education, and the early colleges were closely fashioned after the Oxford and Cambridge pattern, in which divinity and the "humanities" held the first place. The settlers of Massachusetts were men who had fought and suffered for their religious opinions, and they naturally held them with considerable firmness, as opposed to the Church of England on the one hand, and the Baptists and Quakers on the other. So long as the influence of the Pilgrims and their descendants was predominant, it was natural that the affairs of the soul should be uppermost; and not until politics began to interest the colonists in a vital manner did religious books and tracts cease to form the bulk of the issues of the press. Novels and plays were unknown; poetry was didactic, devotional, or satirical; histories were prejudiced by the theological opinions of their writers; and philosophy became an important study only as a means of religious defense. One of the very first issues of the printing-press set up at Cambridge in 1639 was the *Bay Psalm Book*, a metrical version mainly written by New England divines. This was the first book written and printed at home, for though George Sandys, an English gentleman connected with the Virginia company, had made, on the banks of the James River, a tolerable translation of Ovid, he printed it in London.

3. INCREASE AND COTTON MATHER. — Nearly every minister who had anything to say and the means of getting it printed wrote a pamphlet or two. The titles were often of great length. *The Application of Redemption by the Effectual Work of the Word and Spirit of Christ* was as brief as the average; and the interest excited in such works is shown by the fact that this treatise reached a second edition after the death of the author, the Rev. Thomas Hooker, the founder of Hartford. Of all the theological writers of the seventeenth and eighteenth centuries Increase Mather and his son Cotton were the most voluminous. The publications of the former numbered eighty-five, and of the latter no less than three hundred and eighty-two. Increase Mather was born at Dorchester, and graduated at Harvard in 1656, though he deemed an additional European training necessary, and took a degree at Dublin two years later. He was president of Harvard between 1685 and 1701, and had some success in his efforts to be preacher, diplomat, and educator at the same time. His writings have little literary value. Cotton Mather inherited all his father's zeal, together with the bookish tastes of his grandfather, John Cotton, of the First Church in Boston. Cotton Mather graduated at Harvard

in 1678, and, having overcome a painful habit of stammering, became his father's colleague in the North Church, Boston, in 1684. The youth was then only twenty-one years of age, but his head had been crammed with as much knowledge as John Milton's. At twelve he was well along in Hebrew, and had mastered the leading Latin and Greek authors; and his daily life was from the first a wonderful piece of systematic machinery. Mather was a firm supporter of the doctrines of extreme Calvinistic theology, and to him devils and angels were as real as his own family. In witchcraft he fully believed, in common with most of the wise men of his time; and his first important book, *Memorable Providences relating to Witchcraft*, appeared in 1689, three years before the Salem executions, which Mather justified. *The Wonders of the Invisible World*, issued in 1693, gives an account of these executions, without any attempt at compassion, or any intimation that human beings, and not evil spirits, were being put to death. And yet this cold, stern man was a life-long worker for sailors, prisoners, Indians, and all the suffering and oppressed. Mather wrote on a multitude of subjects, but the work on which his reputation chiefly rests is the *Magnalia Christi Americana*, published in London in 1702,— a vast storehouse of ecclesiastical, civil, and educational history, together with many biographical sketches. As a collection of facts it is an authority; and in those passages which are colored by the writer's prejudices it is easy to detach the true from the false. Mather died in 1728, and left a great gap in the literature and theology of the time. By his side the other early clergymen of New England, with two exceptions, must take an inferior place, for they equaled him in zeal and fertility, but not in ability.

4. ELIOT'S INDIAN BIBLE. — John Eliot, the "Apostle to the Indians," was born in England and educated at the University of Cambridge, coming to Boston in 1631, and accepting as his life-mission, the next year, the conversion of the Indians, who were evidently, in his opinion, the descendants of the lost tribes of Israel. Having learned the language by the aid of an Indian servant in his family, he began preaching in Nonantum, now Newton, in 1646. Threats did not affect him, and little churches of natives were slowly gathered in the Massachusetts Bay and Plymouth colonies, twenty-four of his converts aiding the industrious Eliot in carrying them on. He had troubles with the colonists, whom he deterred from extirpating the Indians in 1675, and whom he offended by his *Christian Commonwealth*, published in England in 1660, — a work against which seditious intent was charged. Eliot wrote an English harmony of the Gospels, an Indian grammar, and some lesser works; but his chief monument

of industry and scholarship is his translation of the entire Bible into the Indian tongue. This appeared in two parts, the New Testament in 1661, and the whole Bible in 1663, and was the labor of the unaided Eliot. Its dialect is now unknown save to an antiquary or two. This work is also noticeable as the first Bible, in any language, printed in British America, and still remains the most remarkable contribution to philology made in this country, though its value as a Christianizing agent was of course temporary.

5. ROGER WILLIAMS. — The Pilgrims, although they were in a majority, and controlled religious and social affairs in New England with an iron hand, were not without opponents. Of these, Roger Williams, a Church of England clergyman who had become a non-conformist just before sailing for America, in 1630, was the most prominent. For five years he was in every way a political and theological thorn in the side of the colony, though many of his principles were thoroughly in accord with what is now considered truth and progress. To escape banishment to England he went, with four followers, to the site of the present city of Providence, and set up a community in which secular and religious affairs were divorced. Becoming a Baptist in 1639, he founded a church the same year, which he quitted after a few months. The remainder of his life was mainly spent in Prov-

idence, though he lived in London for some time, where he was surprised to find John Milton as versatile as himself, and considerably more profound. The Quakers were freely admitted to Providence, but Williams and George Fox carried on sharp controversies, and the former willingly engaged in public debate with the Quaker champion. His *Bloody Tenent of Persecution, Hireling Ministry none of Christ's*, and *Experiments of Spiritual Life and Health* are his principal works, but their present value is not great. Williams's whole career shows what a man of sincerity and force can accomplish, though his powers be hindered by a certain instability and superficiality.

6. MINOR WRITERS OF THE SEVENTEENTH CENTURY. — Captain John Smith was a voluminous narrator of his own adventures, telling the story in a simple fashion, but not infrequently inserting statements which were absurdly incorrect. It is supposed that Smith, like some modern travelers, lent his name to the compilations of others, contenting himself with the supply of the unwrought material. Nathaniel Ward, minister at Ipswich, published in 1647 a sharp satire on English social life, called *The Simple Cobbler of Agawam*. Governor John Winthrop's invaluable history of New England, in the form of a journal between 1630 and 1649, was not fully published until 1826. The honor of the first publication of a volume of

poems in New England belongs to Anne Bradstreet, whose collected works appeared in 1678. Some of the poems are by no means devoid of merit, though disfigured by a paucity of words and a stiffness of style. Peter Folger, Benjamin Franklin's grandfather, also wrote a long doggerel entitled *A Looking Glass for the Times*. It was hard to write anything but doggerel so long as the current versions of the Psalms were in vogue. Michael Wigglesworth's *Day of Doom* (1662) is a solemn poem on the day of judgment, with some strong lines, one of which devotes to non-elect infants "the easiest room in hell." It was very popular in its day, running through nine editions in America and two in England.

7. YALE COLLEGE. — In the year 1700 some Connecticut ministers met at New Haven, and talked over the plan of establishing a college in the colony, a subject which had been broached as early as 1647. Meeting again in Branford, the same year, they deposited forty books on a table, each declaring as he laid down his parcel, "I give these books for the founding a college in this colony." In its early years the new institution led a wandering and not altogether peaceful life at Killingworth, Saybrook, and Milford, but was finally located at New Haven, in 1716. The Saybrook Platform (Congregational) had been made binding on the officers in 1708. The religious

teaching of the college was somewhat more conservative than that at Harvard, even in the eighteenth century; but the publications of its officers and graduates were fewer, partly in consequence of the lack of a publishing centre in the colony. Philosophy, however, was from the first a prominent study, and to this fact is due, in some measure, the subsequent career of the most eminent of American metaphysicians.

8. JONATHAN EDWARDS was born in East Windsor, Connecticut, in 1703, graduated at Yale in 1720, was a tutor there between 1724 and 1726, was pastor in Northampton and Stockbridge, and was elected president of the College of New Jersey at Princeton, in 1757, dying there in March of the next year, after holding office less than three months. As a mere youth he began the study of mental science, and took up the task of showing the harmony between the Calvinistic theology and the conclusions of philosophy. Locke he mastered at thirteen, and afterwards studied all other accessible authorities; but Locke's influence was always strong in his mind. In 1746 he wrote a *Treatise on the Religious Affections*, in which he showed what were the marks of true religion. *An Inquiry into the Qualifications for Full Communion* followed; a work in which he laid down the principle, since maintained in the New England Congregational churches, that true conversion and a cor-

rect life should be requisites for admission to the Lord's Supper. This opinion was not shared by his Northampton church, and he was compelled to leave it and accept the duties of missionary to the Stockbridge Indians. In Stockbridge, between 1751 and 1754, he wrote his great treatise on the freedom of the will, the full title of which was *A Careful and Strict Inquiry into the Modern Notion of that Freedom of Will which is supposed to be essential to Moral Agency, Virtue and Vice, Reward and Punishment, Praise and Blame.* His other works were not few, but upon this chiefly rests his reputation as philosopher and theologian. It was designed to show that Calvinistic notions of God's moral government are not contrary to the common sense of mankind, but in strict consonance therewith. Edwards maintained that the will is not self-determined, and that the assertion of absence of certainty in the universe is inconsistent with any correct idea of a ruling power. Some English necessitarians promptly hailed Edwards as one of their number, but he repudiated the connection, and declared that man's sinful disposition was man's greatest sin, far from being an excuse for wrong-doing. From its first appearance until the present time the treatise has been the subject of sharp criticism, both by Calvinists and Arminians, but it has been supported by some of the ablest of American divines.

9. THE FOLLOWERS OF EDWARDS. — The principal leaders, in the eighteenth century, of the school of philosophy which Edwards shaped were Samuel Hopkins, Nathaniel Emmons, and Timothy Dwight. Hopkins studied theology under Edwards, of whom he published a biography. His *System of Theology* appeared in 1793, and "Hopkinsianism" was a common term in New England for many years. Hopkins was one of the first to oppose slavery; he caused it to be abolished in Rhode Island, and formed a plan for colonizing and evangelizing Africa with free negroes. Emmons was pastor of a church in Franklin, Massachusetts, from 1773 to 1840, and his writings were in substantial accord with those of Dr. Hopkins. Timothy Dwight was president of Yale between 1795 and 1817. His *Theology Explained and Defended* (1818) consisted of one hundred and seventy-three sermons. While adhering in the main to the principles of Edwards, he dissented in minor points, and considerably popularized the system. Dr. Dwight, who was one of the most accomplished scholars of his time, also wrote poetry and a book of travels, though his explorations extended no farther than New England and New York.

10. BENJAMIN FRANKLIN. — The eighteenth century had now become rich in the names of great Americans, one of the most remarkable of whom was Benjamin Franklin, who had all the versatility

of Roger Williams and Increase Mather, and was a master in whatever branch of learning he touched. Franklin, the fifteenth of a family of seventeen children, was born in Boston in 1706, his father being a tallow-chandler and his mother the daughter of Peter Folger, a man of some literary ability. Early apprenticed to his brother James as a printer, Franklin read everything he could lay hands upon, and was especially fond of Addison's "Spectator," then a great favorite and a novelty. The itch for writing was soon manifest, and he began to print pieces on public affairs in *The New England Courant*, his brother's newspaper. The people read and liked them, but they caused a disagreement with his brother, and in 1723 young Franklin ran away to New York and Philadelphia, where he went to work as a journeyman printer. In 1730 he bought the *Pennsylvania Gazette*, then two years old, and soon became a power in politics, literature, and society. Through his efforts a library was started in Philadelphia in 1731; the American Philosophical Society in 1743, and the Academy of Philadelphia, afterwards the University of Pennsylvania, in 1749. In 1753 he became postmaster-general for the colonies, and was frequently commissioner between them and England. In 1766 he secured the repeal of the obnoxious Stamp Act; in 1775 he went to the Continental Congress; and in 1776 he helped to draft the Declaration of Independence, which he signed. Between that year and 1785 he was employed abroad in various diplomatic functions, returning in time to be a delegate to the Constitutional Convention in 1787. He died at Philadelphia in 1790.

11. FRANKLIN AS A WRITER. — *A Dissertation on Liberty and Necessity* was printed by Franklin in London in 1725, during a temporary residence in that city, being a reply to a work by William Wollaston on which the young printer was setting type. In 1732 Franklin began, in Philadelphia, the publication of *Poor Richard's Almanac*, the issue of which was continued for twenty-five years. "Richard Saunders, Philomath" was the professed author, and Benjamin Franklin was the printer. The principal part of the almanac was a collection of saws and sayings, which were eagerly awaited by the people, and promptly passed into current circulation. The inculcation of practices of prudence and economy was always a leading idea in these maxims, and they had a prompt effect in increasing the amount of spare money in Philadelphia. Besides these, the almanacs contained jocose introductions and doggerel rhymes for each month. The annual sale was about ten thousand copies, but they were so worn out by their homely readers that copies of the earlier issues are scarce. The most of Franklin's other writings consisted of miscellaneous and random, but by no means hasty, papers on political, finan-

cial, social, and scientific subjects, all of which have been preserved. *The Busybody*, a series of essays in Addisonian style, and some ballads written in early life, should also be mentioned. Franklin was an admirable letter-writer, and in his correspondence a perfect picture of the man is presented. If anything further were needed to complete our idea of his personality, it is supplied in his *Autobiography*, lately produced in a complete form.

12. FRANKLIN AS A SCIENTIST AND DIPLOMATIST. — To Franklin belongs the honor of showing that lightning is electricity, and the invention of the lightning-rod. About the year 1750 he foreshadowed this discovery in his letters, and was elected a fellow of the Royal Society in consequence of his papers on the subject. In foreign courts his influence was largely due to personal power, but as a political writer he is clear and cogent.

13. MINOR WRITERS OF THE EIGHTEENTH CENTURY. — An excellent *History of the First Discovery and Settlement of Virginia* was published in 1747 by William Stith, afterwards president of William and Mary College. David Brainerd, a missionary to the Indians of New England and New York, kept a diary, which was issued after his death, and is an interesting history of the life of a sensitive, industrious, and devout man. These memoirs were edited by Jonathan Edwards. John Woolman, an itinerant Quaker born in New Jersey, wrote little,

his principal literary production being, like Brainerd's, in the form of personal recollections. His *Journal of Life and Travels in the Service of the Gospel* appeared in 1774, three years after his death. It is a charming book, not only as a record of the doings of a singularly innocent and righteous man, but also as a model of literary style. Woolman's unconscious frankness is sometimes amusing, but pathos and humor go hand in hand in his diary. William Livingston, journalist, governor of New Jersey, and member of the Continental Congress and the Constitutional Convention, wrote in 1747 a placid didactic poem on *Philosophic Solitude.*

CHAPTER II.

1775–1812.

1. THE REVOLUTIONARY PERIOD. — The American Revolution was the cause of much commotion in literature as well as in politics, being preceded, attended, and followed by great activity of the pen. A large part of the books and pamphlets written at the time were necessarily of temporary interest and of slight value as literature. But such of the speeches, delivered during or before the meeting of the Continental Congress, as have come down to us are marked by the fire and intensity of an earnest period. James Otis, of Boston, born in 1725, was the author of some vigorous pamphlets, and was a wonderful orator. A few fragments of his speeches have been preserved, but the one which is most familiar to school-boys is an avowed modern imitation. Josiah Quincy, Jr. (1744–1775), shared with Otis, in Massachusetts, the oratorical honors of the time. John Adams wrote some powerful pamphlets, and Patrick Henry, like Otis, deserves literary mention for the fervid eloquence and artistic finish of his speeches. Henry edited an edition of Bishop Butler's "Analogy of Religion."

2. GEORGE WASHINGTON AS A WRITER. — Though Washington wrote little and never paid particular attention to the arts of rhetoric, he was the master of a clear and somewhat individual style. Without including many productions of special interest, his literary remains are sufficient to fill twelve large volumes. The journal of his expedition to the Ohio River was published at Williamsburg, Virginia, in 1754, and his *Farewell Address* in 1796, — a production which would alone entitle the author to mention among American authors. The rest of his collected works consist of addresses, messages, and correspondence. As a letter-writer Washington excelled, like Franklin; and during his life-time he was compelled to make out a list of spurious letters attributed to him, the popularity of his correspondence having led to such forgeries.

3. THOMAS JEFFERSON was probably the best educated man of his time, having been fortunate in his instructors and zealous in the prosecution of his studies. Many branches of learning he had pursued beyond the usual limit, and he excelled in literary composition, though he was no orator. His *Notes on Virginia* were written for the information of the French government, and were published in 1784. They include many shrewd observations and interesting suggestions. Jefferson's somewhat voluminous correspondence may be considered his most graceful literary monument, though the Dec-

laration of Independence, which he wrote, will always be considered one of the most remarkable of public documents, aside from its political importance.

4. THE FEDERALIST was a collection of essays published periodically, and arguing in favor of the Constitution of the United States, adopted in 1789. There were eighty-five numbers in all, of which the first seventy-six appeared in *The Independent Journal*, a semi-weekly newspaper published in New York. The publication began on October 27, 1787, and ceased, as far as the journal was concerned, on April 2, 1788. *The Federalist* was the concerted work of Alexander Hamilton, James Madison, and John Jay, who adopted no separate signatures, but wrote over the common signature of Publius. The letters were addressed to the people of New York, in order to induce that State to support the proposed national Constitution. The purpose of the publication was controversial, for the Constitution had been so sharply attacked that its friends perceived the necessity of rallying to its defense. The original idea was Hamilton's, and he drew up the plan of the series. The completed work does not form a systematic treatise, but covers many questions of government which every student of political science must consider. The authors had a special end in view, and they were zealous to show the colonists that advantage and danger united in de-

manding the adoption of a Federal Constitution. In the light of later experience the wisdom and forethought of the writers are apparent. The work has been repeatedly issued, and is recognized as a standard authority on the elementary principles of government.

5. THOMAS PAINE was a prominent figure in Revolutionary literature. Born in England in 1737, he started in life as a stay-maker and dissenting preacher, meanwhile getting a general knowledge of literature by such promiscuous reading as he could do at odd moments. Becoming angry with the British government in consequence of his dismissal from the revenue service, he came to America in 1774 and obtained speedy notoriety as a political writer. His *Serious Thoughts on Slavery* was a magazine article printed in 1775. *Common Sense*, a political pamphlet, advocating a declaration of independence and the formation of a republic, had a vast circulation, and exerted no small influence. At the end of 1776 Paine started a periodical called *The Crisis*, which was published, at no stated interval, for some time, and had a multitude of readers. His patriotic services during the war were appreciated and rewarded, though his temper got him into occasional trouble. *The Rights of Man*, a vindication of the French Revolution, appeared in 1791 and 1792, and he wrote *The Age of Reason* in 1794 and 1795, partly in a French prison. The

latter work has always had a wide circulation, chiefly among the lower classes. It advocates a pure deism, but its method of criticism and temper of attack are now generally repudiated by more scholarly writers of the same school.

6. POETS. — Philip Freneau, a Huguenot by descent and a New Yorker by birth, was the first American poet to attain eminence, though there were a multitude of anonymous ballad-writers during the war. Freneau graduated at the College of New Jersey in 1771, studying at that institution with James Madison. He published four volumes, and his political burlesques were very popular during the war. Probably he was the first American poet to find readers in England. John Trumbull's *Progress of Dullness* and *Elegy on the Times* attracted no great attention; but his *McFingal* (1782), a satirical poem in the style of Butler's "Hudibras," had a great circulation. Some of its lines are still popularly assigned to Butler. Francis Hopkinson and Robert Treat Paine, Jr., were other patriotic and humorous versifiers. Joel Barlow's *Vision of Columbus* (1787) was for a time a favorite, and his graver *Columbiad*, an expansion of the preceding, issued in 1808, was the first attempt at a national epic. It is stiff and stately, but occasionally rises into merit. Barlow is better known by a poem on "hasty-pudding." Phillis Wheatley, a Massachusetts negress, published a volume of

verse in London in 1773 ; and Dr. James McClurg, of Virginia, wrote graceful poems of compliment. But all the American poetry of the time, even the most patriotic, was in humble imitation of English models.

7. THE FIRST NOVELIST. — Charles Brockden Brown's *Wieland*, printed in 1798, introduced fiction into American literature. The slow appearance of the novel was not strange, for, with the exception of De Foe, the English novelists themselves had failed to win much celebrity before the latter half of the eighteenth century. *Ormond* was Brown's second novel, and the two books received prompt approval. *Arthur Mervyn*, the third novel, was equally successful, and a better story than either. All Brown's stories are told in a graphic style, and their author had no lack of imagination. Later writers have supplanted him, and the prevailing impression of gloom left by his books has not served to make them permanent favorites. Brown, it should be added, started a monthly magazine, and was the first of our authors to make his whole living out of literature.

8. HISTORIANS AND OTHER WRITERS. — The histories written during the last century are chiefly useful as authorities for later writers. David Ramsay prepared many works of value. Jeremy Belknap wrote a *History of New Hampshire* and a useful series of biographies. Hannah Adams's *History of*

New England was the first standard book written by a New England woman, but its merit does not leave this fact as its only distinction. Dr. Abiel Holmes's *Annals of America* is highly valued as a systematic compilation of leading events. In biography, William Wirt wrote a readable life of Patrick Henry; and Chief Justice John Marshall prepared a standard life of Washington. John Ledyard, a daring explorer, started the fashion for travel by publishing the records of his exploits. Scientific research was given a start by the writings of Dr. Benjamin Rush in medicine, Alexander Wilson in ornithology, Samuel Latham Mitchill in chemistry, Benjamin Smith Barton in botany, and Benjamin Thompson, Count Rumford, in physics. Some of the writers of this time would not attract attention nowadays, and not all, even, of those here mentioned, wrote as well as later authors whose names will be necessarily omitted in this book. Washington Irving once jocosely said of himself that he attracted attention because Englishmen were surprised to see an American with a quill in his hand and not on his head. But greater credit always belongs to the pioneer; and it must be remembered that many authors of the eighteenth century wrote with meagre libraries, with a slender reading public to address, with no possibility of making literature a livelihood, and with greater competition from foreign sources than that of which complaint is still made.

CHAPTER III.

1812–1861.

1. THEOLOGICAL CHANGES. — The increasing importance of political affairs, together with the growth in size and prosperity of the whole nation, served to deprive theology of its preëminent place in American literature, though only the relative number of volumes on religious subjects was diminished. The beginning of the present century, however, was marked by a considerable controversial excitement among the New England clergy, incident to the spread of Unitarian views in and around Boston. Harvard University was the centre of interest, and the election of a Unitarian to the Hollis professorship of divinity in that institution, in 1805, excited great attention. The change in the Congregational churches of Massachusetts had been a gradual one, for, as James Russell Lowell has pointed out, many of the Congregational divines of Boston and Cambridge had been regarded with suspicion by their stricter brethren, even during the eighteenth century. In 1785, the very year of the appearance of the first American Episcopal prayer-book, King's Chapel, in Boston,

the pioneer Episcopal society in New England, had stricken out all Trinitarian expressions from its liturgy; while as early as 1718 an Arian had been ordained over the Hingham church. The war of pamphlets and books began in 1812, simultaneously with the second conflict between England and the United States. The Unitarian leaders were William Ellery Channing, the Henry Wares, father and son, and Andrews Norton; while the conservative Congregationalists were championed by Noah Worcester, of Salem, and Moses Stuart and Leonard Woods, professors in the theological seminary at Andover. *The Panoplist* was established as the Trinitarian and *The Christian Examiner* as the Unitarian organ; and the discussion was carried on with great ability on both sides, and with a suitable degree of courtesy, though it was impossible to debate matters in which the nature of God and the destiny of the soul were concerned without considerable earnestness of language. In later years Lyman Beecher, the Alexanders, and Professor Charles Hodge, of the Presbyterian seminary at Princeton, William G. T. Shedd, of Andover Seminary, President Hopkins, of Williams College, Dr. Nehemiah Adams, of Boston, Dr. John Todd, of Pittsfield, and Professor Edwards A. Park, of Andover, have written in defence of the Trinitarian side. More recent Unitarian writers have been Orville Dewey, William H.

Furness, James Freeman Clarke, Henry W. Bellows, Andrew P. Peabody, and William Rounseville Alger. The Unitarians themselves have not desired to keep within their denominational limits such persons as could find greater freedom of thought outside; and Theodore Parker, Cyrus A. Bartol, Moncure D. Conway, and Octavius B. Frothingham, all men of letters, have ceased to work in connection with any organized branch of Christianity. Parker was born at Lexington, Massachusetts, in 1810, was a prodigy of general learning and a marvel of industry, and excelled both as a preacher and a writer. In 1844 he was refused admission to several Unitarian pulpits in Boston, and during that and subsequent years the interest in his extremely radical views caused the last religious excitement which had any general effect on American literature. Parker died at Florence in 1860.

2. WILLIAM ELLERY CHANNING, of the writers we have named, deserves the most prominent mention in a literary history. He was born at Newport in 1780, and although of slight figure and not very firm health, he began to be a hard student at an early age, graduating at Harvard when he was eighteen. His health was then somewhat impaired, and he went to Virginia as a teacher; but the return voyage, in 1800, was so severe that he remained a permanent invalid all his life. In 1803

he became pastor of a Boston church, and soon was famous as a finished orator. His style was nothing less than charming, and his *Remarks on the Life and Character of Napoleon Bonaparte*, published in 1828, gave him a European reputation. Many of his sermons were published, and he was continually giving addresses at ordinations and literary anniversaries, which occasions he used to make notable by the presentation of carefully prepared opinions on the leading religious and political questions of the time. He had returned from Virginia an uncompromising opponent of slavery, and he argued against it to the day of his death. Strange to say, he paid no attention to literary composition, and hated controversy; but his opinions were firmly established and his method of expression straightforward; so that his writings have a strong sweep. He had no need to remember even the old maxim, that art is to conceal art; for he spoke and wrote in the simplest and most natural way, and was surprised to find himself considered eloquent. His ideas of the sacredness of conscience were almost superstitious, and he thought the rights of the pleader ended with the solicitation toward obedience to the dictates of one's own sense of duty. His literary papers show what his reputation would have been had he confined himself to polite letters. His works fill six volumes, and are still found worthy of study, for they retain a considerable pop ularity in America and England, despite the temporary character of most of the subjects of the various lectures and essays. Channing died in 1842, at the age of sixty-two.

3. OTHER THEOLOGICAL WRITERS. — It will be best to finish at this place the enumeration of the other leading religious writers of the century. The principal theological work that has appeared since Edwards's famous treatise is the *Systematic Theology* of Charles Hodge, professor in Princeton seminary. Dr. Hodge was born in Philadelphia in 1797; graduated at Princeton in 1815; and was connected with the seminary from 1820 to 1878. He founded a review in 1825, which is still published, and which for half a century supported the Presbyterian tenets of faith. A few commentaries, a Presbyterian church history, and a religious manual preceded the extensive work previously mentioned, which appeared in 1871 and 1872. No abler exposition of Calvinistic principles has been made since Edwards, and Dr. Hodge covered more ground than his predecessor. The whole treatise is carefully elaborated, and represents the patient labor of a life-time. James McCosh, who became president of Princeton College in 1868, had won a reputation as a philosopher and theologian before his departure from Belfast, Ireland. But since he has made the United States his home, mention should be made of the principal works he has published in this

country. They are *The Laws of Discursive Thought* (1869); *Christianity and Positivism* (1871), a reply to the school of John Stuart Mill; and *The Scottish Philosophy* (1874), a popular history, defense, and exposition of the metaphysical school to which the author belongs. Two other college presidents — Mark Hopkins of Williams and Noah Porter of Yale — have devoted much thought and ability to mental science. Dr. Hopkins's influence has been personal, to a considerable extent, but his *Evidences of Christianity* and *Law of Love* have put his arguments before the outside world. Dr. Porter is the author of a larger work on *The Human Intellect*, an elaborate and thorough manual of philosophy, of which the author has prepared an abridgment. Thomas C. Upham, professor in Bowdoin College, wrote in 1831 a work on the *Elements of Mental Philosophy*, long the principal text-book on the subject in American schools. James Marsh, president of the University of Vermont between 1826 and 1833, exerted considerable influence in popularizing the transcendental philosophy of Coleridge in this country, though his writings were fragmentary. Laurens P. Hickok, long connected with Union College, Schenectady, has expounded in several works the doctrine of "the necessary distinctions in the intellectual functions of the sense, the understanding, and the reason," — the quotation is from President Seelye of Amherst, — and this doctrine he chiefly elaborated in his latest work, *The Logic of Reason*. His literary style is obscure. Francis Wayland, president of Brown University, Providence, from 1827 to 1855, wrote excellent textbooks of ethics, philosophy, and political economy (from the free-trade standpoint). Tayler Lewis, professor in Union College, was linguist, philosopher, and scientist; and, though holding opinions of the stoutest orthodoxy, foreshadowed in *Science and the Bible* (1857) some of the results of later biological investigations. Philip Schaff, a native of Switzerland, who came to the United States in 1844, has written the early volumes of a projected *History of the Christian Church*, and has been an industrious editor of Lange's extended commentary on the Bible, as well as of the principal creeds of Christendom. Another leading work in church history is Professor W. G. T. Shedd's *History of Christian Doctrine* (Calvinistic), against which W. R. Alger's radical *History of the Doctrine of the Future Life*, may be matched in ability, though hardly in dignity. Denominational histories have been prepared for the Episcopalians by Bishop William Stevens Perry; for the Congregationalists by George Punchard and Henry M. Dexter; for the Presbyterians by E. H. Gillett; and for the Methodists by Abel Stevens. Of these the last is the most noticeable. George Bush, Henry James, and Theophilus Parsons have expounded Swedenborgian doctrines. Drs. T. J.

Conant of the Baptists, Albert Barnes of the Presbyterians, John McClintock of the Methodists, and Ezra Abbot of the Unitarians have been experts in biblical study. Few notable works from Roman Catholic sources have appeared, though Archbishops Martin J. Spalding and John Hughes were forcible and somewhat voluminous writers. A foundation for lectures on preaching at the Yale Theological Seminary has given our literature an excellent little library of works on homiletics, in which volumes have appeared by Henry Ward Beecher, John Hall, William M. Taylor, and Phillips Brooks. Mr. Beecher has been, both in the pulpit and the press, an active supporter of the more liberal Congregational ideas, and his miscellaneous publications cover a wide range. The other principal exponents of less stringent views in the historic New England theology have been Drs. Nathaniel W. Taylor, of Yale, President Charles G. Finney, of Oberlin, and Horace Bushnell, of Hartford. Dr. Bushnell wrote *God in Christ, Nature and the Supernatural, The Vicarious Sacrifice,* and other works, chiefly in defense of a "moral influence" theory of the atonement, and written with much ripeness of thought and beauty of style. And so we close the long list of later theologians. We have seen that, to the last, philosophy has been mainly regarded as a defense and illustration of theology, and that American metaphysics have been, in consequence, at once less brilliant and less destructive than English or German. This record now returns to the miscellaneous literature of the country, which had made but a modest figure before the second war with England.

4. THE KNICKERBOCKER SCHOOL. — "The Knickerbocker writers" is a loose and not very useful term applied to certain authors who began to write soon after the beginning of the century, who were for the most part residents of New York, and who were in some cases descendants of the old Dutch stock. After the *Knickerbocker Magazine* was established some of them became its contributors, and this fact caused the nickname to cling longer than it otherwise would have done. For the sake of convenience the members of the coterie may be considered in order, including under this head the names of Washington Irving, James Kirke Paulding, Joseph Rodman Drake, and Fitz-Greene Halleck.

5. WASHINGTON IRVING was a native of New York city, born in 1783, and growing up in familiarity with its sights and characteristics. His father was of an old Scotch family, and his mother was an Englishwoman. They were married before coming to this country. The boy's older brothers had rather marked literary tastes, and under their guidance and example he soon began to read such of the English authors as his father's library con-

tained. At nineteen he wrote for a newspaper edited by his brother Peter, taking up theatrical and social topics, and using the name of Jonathan Oldstyle. This pseudonym describes the nature and tone of these youthful productions with sufficient accuracy. In 1804, attacked by a slight malady of the lungs, Irving sailed for Bordeaux, whence, after various tours in the Mediterranean and Italy, he went to Paris for a few months' residence. Taking Belgium and Holland on the way, he next settled for a time in London. Washington Allston, the painter, he met in Rome, and half made up his mind to abandon literature for art. He returned to New York in 1806, with a wide European experience and a great store of literary material. At home again, he at once set himself to work, and the next year started a fortnightly periodical after the style of the English essayists of the eighteenth century. *Salmagundi* was the title, and it professed to give the "whim-whams and opinions of Launcelot Langstaff, Esquire." Like Addison, Irving had the help of other literary friends in his enterprise, Paulding aiding him in the prose and his brother William furnishing the poetry. The social follies and fashions of the day were satirized in a vein of genial humor, and the work is therefore a good picture of bygone customs. There is a story running through the whole, and most of the characters mentioned were real persons. Cockloft Hall, which figured prominently in the periodical, was a fine old house (still standing, though so modernized as to be unrecognizable) on the bank of the Passaic River, in Newark. In December, 1809, *Knickerbocker's History of New York* appeared. Washington Irving and Peter Irving began it as a parody on a popular handbook issued a short time before, and its historical style was a burlesque of the language of a sketch printed in that publication. When Peter Irving went to Europe, Washington determined to continue the historical burlesque, and to make it a longer and independent comic history. An air of verisimilitude was given it by the publication of some preliminary notices concerning the finding of the manuscript in the Columbian Hotel, in Mulberry Street; and not a few persons were dull enough to be deceived by its evident but very delicate pleasantry. Some descendants of the Dutchmen took serious offense at the personal caricatures in the book, but everybody read it, and it was not long before it became a national classic. We had, at length, something all our own, which was not copied from London or borrowed from Paris; and the impetus thus given to native production was very great. In 1810 Irving wrote a short biographical sketch of the poet Campbell, and three years later edited a magazine in Philadelphia, which for the next few years showed some signs of becoming the literary capital of the country. During another trip to Europe he began to publish the *Sketch Book*, in numbers, and it was a success both in London and New York. Irving had won the warm friendship of Sir Walter Scott, who induced the London publisher, Murray, to accept his book and pay the round price of £200 for it. Murray afterwards doubled this sum, and Irving soon found himself in receipt of revenues from his pen much greater than Charles Brockden Brown, his only American predecessor as a professional author, ever enjoyed. The *Sketch Book* contained the *Legend of Sleepy Hollow* and *Rip Van Winkle;* and readers perceived that a new master of prose style had arisen, as well as a delicate humorist and a man in sympathy with the human heart. In 1820 and 1821 Irving was in Paris, and in the latter year Murray paid him the enormous price of £1,000 for *Bracebridge Hall*, a collection of stories and sketches. In 1824 £1,500 was paid by the same publisher for the *Tales of a Traveller*, a work of similar character, and containing stories of greater interest. Strange to say, it met with sharp criticism both in England and the United States. Two years later Alexander H. Everett, then minister to Spain, gave Irving a commission to translate some recently collected documents concerning Columbus. This was the basis of Irving's *Life and Voyages of Christopher Columbus*, published in London in 1828, which was sold for three thousand guineas. Irving was now as successful both in fame and money, as the best English authors, who wrote at that period of high literary remuneration. This biographical work was kindly received by the critics, and seems to have determined Irving to cultivate the Spanish field further. The *Chronicles of the Conquest of Granada* followed, the author having made another tour in the south of Spain. It was a losing venture, and attracted no general praise; but Irving wrote still another Spanish book in the *Voyages of the Companions of Columbus*, which appeared in 1831. *The Alhambra* (1832) was a sort of Spanish edition of *Bracebridge Hall*. After serving for a time as secretary of legation in London, Irving returned home in 1832, received a public dinner, and determined to explore the wilds of the West, in lieu of Castilian antiquities. His *Tour on the Prairies* (1835) was issued, with some European sketches, in a volume entitled *The Crayon Miscellany*, which took its name from the author's pseudonym of Geoffrey Crayon, Gentleman. *Astoria*, the obscurest of his books, described Irving's youthful visits to the Montreal station of the Northwest Fur Company, and embodied accounts of early fur-trading expeditions in Oregon, by John Jacob Astor and others. Miscellaneous contributions to the *Knickerbocker Magazine* occupied the author until his appointment, in 1842, as minister to Spain. Coming back in 1846, he enlarged a very agreeable biography of Oliver Goldsmith, in which he hit Dr. Johnson some hard raps, and also went to work on *Mahomet and his Successors*, published in 1850. About the same time he subjected the whole of his previous works to slight revisions, and a new and uniform edition was brought out. Undeterred by advancing age (he was now 67), Irving set to work upon his largest labor, the *Life of Washington*, the fifth and last volume of which was published three months before his death, in 1859. This work had an army of readers, and deserved them, for it embodied all the accessible facts concerning Washington's life, in the felicitous style of one of the greatest masters of English. The earlier works, however, are most prized by the author's public, and the *Sketch Book*, on the whole, remains the best example of his powers, combining, as it does, humor, pathos, and a wonderful felicity of description. Irving never married, but kept bachelor's hall in an attractive fashion at his cottage of "Sunnyside," in Tarrytown.

6. JAMES KIRKE PAULDING was five years older than Irving, having been born in 1778 in the town of Nine Partners, in Dutchess County, New York. He also survived Irving for a similarly brief period, dying in Hyde Park, New York, in 1860. William Irving was his brother-in-law, and Paulding took up his abode in the house of that gentleman,

in New York, in 1797. Of course, having literary tastes of his own, he fell in heartily with the plans of his every-day associates, and worked upon *Salmagundi* with enthusiasm, when that short-lived periodical was started. Paulding was an office-holder a good part of his life, being secretary to the board of navy commissioners in 1815, navy agent at New York for a dozen years, and secretary of the navy during the administration of Van Buren. He began his career as a poet; brought out, single-handed, in 1819, a second series of *Salmagundi;* and during all his life was constantly writing poems, novels, humorous sketches, and pamphlets. *The Dutchman's Fireside*, a novel published in 1831, is his best work; though, like Irving, he wrote a considerable life of Washington. Paulding's mark on American literature was not a permanent one, though sufficient interest remained in his writings to warrant the publication of a revised edition of the best of them in 1867 and 1868.

7. JOSEPH RODMAN DRAKE was a sort of American Keats in that he wrote little, died young, and has kept a permanent place in the standard library. At the time of his death (1820) he was only twenty-five, having been a resident of New York all his life. Poverty was his lot at the first, but he contrived to study medicine, taking his degree in 1816. Marrying a rich wife was his deliverance, and he was thus enabled to spend much of his time with

Fenimore Cooper and Fitz-Greene Halleck, meanwhile maturing plans for literary labor. *The Culprit Fay*, his chief work, appeared in 1819, having been written in consequence of a discussion between Drake, Cooper, and Halleck concerning the poetry of American rivers. In 1819, having been to Europe, he united with Halleck to contribute satirical verses to the newspapers, under the name of "Croaker," or "Croaker, Jr." *The American Flag*, a national lyric of much spirit, keeps Drake's name in the school readers. He died of consumption in 1820, thus completing the parallel to Keats. It is useless to speculate on the possibilities of his career had he lived; but surely none of our poets, unless it be Bryant, wrote so well while yet under age.

8. FITZ-GREENE HALLECK was almost exactly a contemporary of Irving and Paulding, having been born at Guilford, Connecticut, in 1790, and dying there in 1867. He removed to New York in 1811, and became clerk in a banking-house, but afterwards went into the office of John Jacob Astor. Halleck, Charles Sprague, Hiram Rich, and Edmund C. Stedman, of our poets, have resembled the English Samuel Rogers in being connected with banking. Halleck wrote little poems when a boy, some of which he contrived to get printed in the newspapers. But when he formed his literary partnership with Drake, though twenty-eight years

old, he had no great reputation. He wrote little more than Drake, and his magnificent *Marco Bozzaris* (first published in a volume in 1827) has remained his virtual title to fame, though he wrote a long poem called *Fanny*, and lesser pieces entitled *Alnwick Castle* and *Burns*, which have their admirers. On Drake's death he produced an excellent poem, four lines of which promptly passed into the paradise of current quotation. With the mention of his poem on *Twilight*, it is only necessary to add that Halleck retired to Guilford in 1849 on a pension of two hundred dollars a year, given by the will of John Jacob Astor. Halleck edited an excellent edition of Byron, as well as two volumes of selections from the British poets.

9. OTHER EARLY POETS. — Richard Henry Dana was born in 1787, and in early life, having studied at Harvard, was associated with the club of gentlemen, headed by William Tudor, which established *The North American Review* in 1815. Oddly, the the venerable Mr. Dana did not receive his degree of Bachelor of Arts until 1866, at the age of seventy-eight, having participated in the famous Harvard rebellion of 1807. Like his New York contemporaries, he published an essay-serial called *The Idle Man*, on which Bryant and Washington Allston gave him some help. *The Buccaneer*, with other excellent and carefully written poems, appeared in 1827, and this piece remains his best

achievement. His prose essays are graceful and his poetical style worthy of comparison with that of the British poets of the elder day. Charles Sprague, a Bostonian who never went ten miles from his home, was another writer who deserves mention for the quality rather than the quantity of his verse. His *Ode on Shakespeare* is a remarkable and admirable production. Richard Henry Wilde, a native of Dublin and a member of Congress from Georgia, wrote a good *Life of Tasso*, a long poem entitled *Hesperia*, and a famous lyric beginning, *My Life is like a Summer Rose*. Other poets made celebrated by single pieces were Francis Scott Key, whose *Star Spangled Banner* was written during the siege of Fort McHenry, Baltimore, in the war of 1812; Samuel Woodworth, who wrote *The Old Oaken Bucket;* John Howard Payne, whose *Home, Sweet Home* was first made public in a play; Albert G. Greene, the author of *Old Grimes is Dead;* and William Augustus Muhlenberg, whose *I would not live alway* is one of the most famous of hymns. Washington Allston, the artist, wrote some rather frivolous poems and a tolerably good novel. J. G. C. Brainard and James A. Hillhouse were the successors of Trumbull in Connecticut. Hillhouse was the author of somewhat heavy poems and dramas on religious subjects, *Hadad* coming under the latter head, and being his best-known production.

10. WILLIAM CULLEN BRYANT connected the earlier and later days of our literature; for, unlike Mr. Dana, he continued his activity as an author to the end of his life, in 1878. He was born in Cummington, Massachusetts, in 1794, his father being the village physician and a man of good mental powers. Of all examples of literary precocity Bryant is the most remarkable. At the age of ten he was writing verse for the country papers, and at fourteen he brought out a couple of political poems, *The Embargo* and *The Spanish Revolution*. They were received with such favor that it was difficult to persuade the public that they were the work of a boy of fourteen. A second edition appeared in 1809, with certifications to that effect. In 1810 Bryant entered Williams College, but did not graduate, receiving, like Dana, his bachelor's degree many years afterward. While in college he was famous as a writer and reader. Taking the law for his profession, he printed in 1816 his celebrated poem of *Thanatopsis*, choosing as the vehicle *The North American Review*, which began as a bi-monthly and a general literary magazine. The poem has since been greatly changed, but even in its earliest form it plainly showed the arrival of an American poet greater than any who had preceded him. Though the poem has death for its subject, it contains, like the Psalms of David, no absolute expression concerning the conscious immortality of

the soul; yet it has been universally accepted by Christians as an embodiment of right views of life and death; omitting, perhaps, but not denying. In 1821 Bryant read a long poem on *The Ages*, before the Phi Beta Kappa Society at Harvard, and the same year collected a few of his poems in a volume published at Cambridge. In 1825 he removed to New York, and became editor of the *United States Review*, for which he wrote largely. The next year he became editorially connected with the *Evening Post*, then a strong Federalist paper, but changed by Bryant into an organ of Democracy and free trade. A little bound volume, called *The Talisman*, appeared annually for three years, beginning in 1827, Robert C. Sands and Gulian C. Verplanck doing some of the writing, and Bryant the rest. It only differed from *The Idle Man* and *Salmagundi* in its wider scope, less frequent issue, and possession of covers. At this time Bryant wrote occasional short stories. In 1832 he brought out a new edition of his poems, which, thanks to the influence of Irving, was reissued in London. Kit North praised it in "Blackwood," and the poet's position became secure, both abroad and at home. Between 1834 and 1849 Bryant was thrice in Europe, and wrote of his journeyings in a prose work called *Letters of a Traveller*. A second series of these letters followed another journey in 1858. By 1864 Mr. Bryant, though a very slow and painstaking writer, had accumulated enough additional poems to make a thin volume. Of all his pieces, besides *Thanatopsis*, those entitled *To a Waterfowl*, *A Forest Hymn*, and *The Planting of the Apple-Tree* are the best. Bryant is the poet of nature, whose various moods are accurately depicted in his polished verse. A certain coldness can fairly be charged against him, but no underlying lack of human sympathy. After passing his seventieth birthday, he determined to translate the *Iliad* of Homer. Although, unlike certain other celebrated translators, he was not compelled to learn the language, he prepared himself thoroughly for the task, and published in 1869 a version which, notwithstanding the constant agitation in England, for twenty years, of the question of Homeric translation, has been very generally accepted as the best English Homer. It is in unrhymed heroic pentameter. A similar translation of the *Odyssey* appeared in 1871. By a fortunate circumstance, the short period since 1867 has seen the appearance in America of new versions of the *Iliad*, *Odyssey*, *Divine Comedy*, *Æneid*, and *Faust*, each of which has at once taken the foremost place among translations in English. Of the last three mention will be made under the names of their respective translators.

11. HENRY WADSWORTH LONGFELLOW is the second in age of the five greater American poets,—

Bryant, Longfellow, Whittier, Holmes, and Lowell, — being ten months older than Whittier, though both were born in 1807. Longfellow was born in Portland, Maine, of a courtly and well-to-do family. When fourteen years old he entered Bowdoin College, where he graduated in 1825 in the class with Nathaniel Hawthorne. It is a circumstance without precedent that the two persons who are by many considered the first poet and the first prose writer of the country received their bachelor's degree at the same time and from the same hands. Other members of this remarkable class were George B. Cheever, John S. C. Abbott, and S. S. Prentiss. William Pitt Fessenden, John P. Hale, and Franklin Pierce were also in college at the time. Like Bryant, Longfellow at first determined to be a lawyer, but the year after graduation, though but nineteen, he was offered the professorship of modern languages at Bowdoin, to qualify himself for which position he spent three years of study in Europe. From 1829, after his return, until 1835 he occupied the chair, writing short poems, and printing prose articles in the *North American Review*. His first book was a little essay on the moral and devotional poetry of Spain, including translations of the *Coplas de Manrique* and some of Lope de Vega's sonnets. In 1835 he was chosen to succeed George Ticknor, who had just resigned the chair of modern languages at Harvard, a position in filling which the university authorities have always shown remarkable wisdom. This professorship he continued to hold until 1854, when he resigned and was succeeded by James Russell Lowell. With occasional trips to Europe, he has since resided in Cambridge, occupying the stately old house used by Washington for his head-quarters in 1775.

12. LONGFELLOW'S POEMS. — *Voices of the Night*, his first original volume, appeared in 1839, and included the best of the author's poems written up to that date; among them, some produced in his undergraduate days at Bowdoin. He was luckier than Tennyson in the reception given to his first venture, for *A Psalm of Life*, *The Reaper and the Flowers*, and *Woods in Winter* were among the pieces included, almost every one of which at once became a popular favorite. *Ballads and Other Poems* — among them *The Skeleton in Armor*, *The Rainy Day*, and *The Village Blacksmith* — appeared in 1842; and also a slender collection of *Poems on Slavery*, generally considered the least meritorious of the poet's works. *The Spanish Student* (1843), a capital drama, introduced an element of humor which Mr. Longfellow, with a single exception, did not afterwards cultivate. *The Belfry of Bruges*, mainly original poems, with a few translations, came in 1846. The next year, 1847, Mr. Longfellow began the publication of several poems which

had a powerful effect in stimulating the growth of a literature devoted to American subjects. *Evangeline* was the first, written in hexameters, a metre previously little used. In its employment Mr. Longfellow has had plenty of followers, but none have succeeded in its use save Arthur H. Clough, an English poet who resided in America for a time, and William D. Howells. The latter writer, unlike Longfellow, introduces rhymes into the metre. *The Seaside and the Fireside* (minor poems) and *The Golden Legend* came between *Evangeline* and *Hiawatha* (1855), another American poem, this time on an Indian subject, and written in a second unfamiliar metre, trochaic octosyllables. In it were embodied many Indian legends industriously collected by the author, and put into a form that proved attractive to multitudes of Americans, and wholly novel to the English public, which had already given to Longfellow greater favor than it had ever shown to Tennyson. *The Courtship of Miles Standish* (1858) was a semi-humorous poem of colonial days, also in hexameters. In *Tales of a Wayside Inn* (1863) the expedient was adopted of embodying, as tales told at a chance gathering in an old inn at Sudbury, several long poems on various subjects. Two additional series have since appeared. Mr. Longfellow's distinctively American poems closed with *The New England Tragedies* (1868), two stern colonial dramas; and in 1871, having published *The Divine Tragedy*, a dramatic account of the crucifixion of Christ, the author united the two last-mentioned works and *The Golden Legend* in a single volume entitled *Christus*. They make a symmetrical whole, but the idea of connecting them was probably conceived after the issue of the earliest part. *The Hanging of the Crane*, a brief domestic poem, made a sumptuous illustrated volume in 1874; and the next year the poet read at the fiftieth anniversary of his graduation at Bowdoin a remarkable poem, *Morituri Salutamus*, which, unlike most occasional pieces, was great and noble, because of the author's intense personal feeling in the event. *Flower de Luce*, *Aftermath*, *The Masque of Pandora*, and *Kéramos* are collections of poems contributed during the past dozen years to various periodicals. Throughout all Longfellow's poetry the prevailing marks are grace and beauty, warmed by a greater human sympathy than is displayed in the writings of the majority of eminent poets.

13. LONGFELLOW'S PROSE WORKS. — Though they are only three in all, the prose volumes of Mr. Longfellow deserve to rank with the best of American books. Daintiness is their prevailing characteristic. *Outre-Mer* (1835) is a collection of sketches of travel, with special attention to the romantic features of continental life. *Hyperion* (1839) is a rounded and interesting romance, with

a quaintness which is not artificial. It is a wonderful example of the beauty of the English language. *Kavanagh* (1849) is a shorter tale, written in a more popular, but idyllic, style. It should be mentioned that an essay on Anglo-Saxon literature, published more than forty years ago, gave the first considerable impulse to the study of that language, in which American scholars have since done more work than their English contemporaries.

14. LONGFELLOW'S DANTE. — All through his poetry Mr. Longfellow shows the influence of his familiar acquaintance with foreign literature, and almost all of his collected volumes have contained a few translations. Between 1867 and 1870, a volume a year, appeared his translation of the *Divine Comedy* of Dante, on which he had spent more than thirty years' time. It closely follows the metre of the original, line by line; and may be said to have ended forever the day of the old-fashioned loose school of translators, like Chapman, Dryden, and Pope. The spirit as well as the form of the original is preserved; and Mr. Longfellow, besides giving a version of Dante which is incomparably superior to its predecessors, has influenced, by his work, quite a body of American literalists. This fidelity and sympathy is gained, however, at the expense of tripping ease of language, and the translation must be considered rather hard reading, a circumstance partly due to the frequent presence of the feminine ending of the verse.

15. JOHN GREENLEAF WHITTIER, although always the most industrious and conscientious of authors, never attained high popularity until recent years, when, by common consent, he has been ranked with the first of American poets. A poor boy, of Quaker parentage, he began life as a farm hand and shoemaker, going to the village school in the winter months. His first poetical efforts, written when he was but seventeen, were published in the Newburyport *Free Press*, edited by William Lloyd Garrison, and he subsequently contributed verses to the Haverhill (Masachusetts) *Gazette*, published near his birthplace. He afterwards contrived to spend two years at the academy in that town. In 1829 he began to be connected with journalism in Boston, where, as well as in Hartford, Haverhill, Philadelphia, and Washington, he edited newspapers until 1839, and in 1847 he became corresponding editor of Dr. Gamaliel Bailey's *National Era*, of Washington, to which he contributed many poems, reformatory and otherwise. He early identified himself with the movement for the abolition of slavery, aiding in the establishment of the American Antislavery Society at Philadelphia; and of this act he has said that, though not insensible to literary reputation, he set a higher value on his "name as appended to the Antislavery Declaration of 1833 than on the title-page of any book." *Legends of New Eng-*

land (1831) was the title of his first collection of poems, but after that and throughout the long anti-slavery agitation, his poems were chiefly reformatory, and directed to awakening the people to the horrors of slavery and the wickedness of any compromise or complicity with those who were engaged in the dreadful traffic. His *Voices of Freedom* (1841) and *The Panorama and other Poems* (1856) contain many poems which are full of fire and inspiration, and glow with moral indignation and scorn. They were spirit-stirring as a trumpet-blast, and a powerful help towards the downfall of slavery. His poems, *In War-Time* (1863), gave him a popularity which his adherence to the hitherto despised cause had rendered impossible, and with the close of the war he gladly turned his pen to gentler themes, publishing successively *Snow-Bound* (1865), *The Tent on the Beach* (1867), *Among the Hills* (1868), *Miriam* (1870), *The Pennsylvania Pilgrim* (1872), *Hazel-Blossoms* (1874), and *The Vision of Echard* (1878). *Maud Muller* is the best known of his poems on other than political or moral topics, and *Barbara Frietchie* (1862) the most remarkable of those connected with the civil war. *Snow-Bound* is a genuine New England idyl, and puts between its covers more of the spirit of the region than any other American book. It will forever remain a national classic. Mr. Whittier has collected the chief of his prose writings in two volumes, and has edited the best edition of John Woolman's *Journal.* As a writer of prose, he unites strength and grace in an unusual degree. His biographical sketches are valuable as contributions to political history, and, in some cases, beautiful as the tribute of friend to friend.

16. HOLMES'S POEMS. — Oliver Wendell Holmes was born in a historic house in Cambridge, just opposite the Harvard University buildings, in 1809, and grew up in that town before it had outgrown its quainter local characteristics. At twenty he graduated at Harvard, in a class whose virtues and whose ornaments he has never ceased to celebrate in anniversary poems. Like Bryant, Longfellow, and Lowell, he started out as a lawyer, but soon took up medicine, which he studied in Europe, paying special attention to anatomy, which branch he has long taught at Harvard. *The Collegian*, a college periodical, received many contributions from him, and in 1836, the year he took his medical degree, he brought out a collected edition of his poems in Boston, including a rhymed essay on *Poetry*, read by him at Cambridge that year. From that time he has always been the favorite American poet at literary anniversaries. His lyrical facility is greater than that of any other of our writers, and for neatness it is not too much to say that he is the equal of Pope. That he is a humorist has detracted from rather than added to

his reputation, for there is a popular idea that a humorist cannot have deep feeling. In Holmes's case this is not true, for *The Last Leaf*, perhaps his best single poem, is a masterpiece of pathos. *Old Ironsides* is a standard national lyric, and Holmes wrote a good share of the few commendable poems evoked by the civil war. Some of his best pieces — *The Deacon's Masterpiece, Parson Turell's Legacy*, and *Homesick in Heaven* — have first appeared in his longer prose works, where they have fitted into their surroundings with exquisite appropriateness. He has written no long poem.

17. HOLMES'S PROSE WORKS. — Dr. Holmes was a leading spirit in the establishment of *The Atlantic Monthly*, which became, with its first number, the "Blackwood" of Boston, and has probably printed more articles by eminent authors within the past twenty years than any magazine in the language. Its prompt success was principally due to Dr. Holmes's *Autocrat of the Breakfast-Table*, a series of articles, half story, half essay, which were a novelty in American literature. Their satire is severe and yet genial, and their wit is as polished and supple as a Damascus blade. *The Professor at the Breakfast-Table*, written in the same style, soon followed; and in 1872 the author once more tried the dangerous experiment of endeavoring to repeat a former triumph, in which attempt he was entirely successful. *Elsie Venner*, a curious novel whose

burden was inherited tendencies, appeared in 1860, and *The Guardian Angel*, probably the best American novel thus far produced, in 1867. The hero of the latter work is a scholarly old bachelor who has written an unsuccessful book, but who goes through the world like a moving patch of sunshine. Dr. Holmes has further expounded his ideas concerning transmitted characteristics in a tractate on *Mechanism in Thought and Morals* (1871).

18. JAMES RUSSELL LOWELL, like Holmes, has written both poetry and prose, but it will not be necessary to consider them in separate sections. He, too, was born in Cambridge, in 1819, in a spacious old house which is still his home. His father was the minister of the West Congregational Church in Boston. Lowell graduated at Harvard in 1838, when he was class poet, and recited a poem which was memorable in the student literature of the time. A law office in Boston was opened in 1840, but the poet soon shut its doors and devoted himself entirely to literature. *A Year's Life* (1841) included his poems up to that date, some of which the author has since revised, throwing away the rest. Two years later he began the publication, in Boston, of *The Pioneer*, a periodical of so high a character that it would surely fail now, and of course promptly came to its death at that time, though Lowell, Hawthorne, and Poe wrote for it. Robert Carter assisted Lowell in editing the three

numbers that appeared. In 1844 Lowell gathered poems enough to make another volume; among them were *A Legend of Brittany* and *Rhœcus*. Some of the sonnets were pronounced in their antislavery sentiments, being addressed to Wendell Phillips and Joshua R. Giddings. The remainder of the volume consisted of pieces which indicated that a new and true poet had arisen. The subjects were not novel, but they were treated in a style which was a rare union of strength and minuteness of phrase, the author's opulence of thought preventing his nicety from seeming artificial. A prose series of *Conversations on the Old Poets* (1845) critically considered Chaucer, George Chapman, and some obscure writers. It found few readers, and has never been reissued, though its author's maturer judgment has since prepared critical articles on several of the authors included, notably Chaucer. Another volume of poems was printed in 1848, of which *The Present Crisis* made a considerable sensation. *The Vision of Sir Launfal*, published the same year, is the most elaborate of the author's productions, being an allegory of good deeds, and containing many quotable lines. At this time Mr. Lowell was very industrious, for in 1848 he also brought out, in New York, *A Fable for Critics*, a wonderfully clever characterization, in fluent verse, of the leading authors of the day, himself included. This characterization, though made in a humorous style, was accurate and just, and in the case of the younger writers mentioned its predictions have been amply verified. At the same time appeared the first series of the *Biglow Papers*, a collection of poems in Yankee dialect, by " Hosea Biglow," edited and furnished with absurdly learned notes and introductions by "Homer Wilbur, A. M., pastor of the First Church in Jaalam." These poems served a double purpose; that of preserving the perishable local expressions of New England in a permanent form, and of fighting with the sharpest weapons of satire against the extension of slavery. This work, together with the *Fable for Critics*, for the first time made Mr. Lowell a popular author, and gave him a reputation in England, though English readers have more recently discovered that he is something more than a humorist. In 1855 Mr. Lowell succeeded Mr. Longfellow in the chair of polite letters at Harvard, taking a European trip before entering upon his new duties. In 1867 a second series of the *Biglow Papers* included those poems in dialect which had been called out by the war. They were preceded by a critical essay in which was shown the antiquity of many presumed Yankee peculiarities of expression. Never a fertile writer, it was not until 1869 that sufficient minor poems were collected by Mr. Lowell to make another volume, which took its title of *Under the Willows* from its leading poem. The *Commemoration Ode* in honor of the Harvard men who were killed in the war, was recited at Cambridge in 1865, and is the author's noblest poem and the chief literary result of the war. For considerable periods Mr. Lowell was editor of *The Atlantic Monthly* and *The North American Review;* and his critical and miscellaneous essays in those periodicals have been collected into volumes entitled *Among my Books* (two series) and *My Study Windows*. These books, which show their author to be the leading American critic, are a very agreeable union of wit and wisdom, and are the result of extensive reading, illuminated by excellent critical insight. The only objection ever made to them is due to their somewhat colloquial style; but this has been generally regarded as one of their charms. As literary guides and stimulants for young readers they are unsurpassed.

19. EDGAR ALLAN POE was an entirely original figure in American literature. His temperament was melancholy; he hated restraint of every kind; and he was the slave of drink. These three circumstances made his life a wretched record of poverty and suffering. But his *Bells*, *Raven*, and *Annabel Lee* are wonderfully melodious; and he was a master in that assonance and alliteration which have since been so marked a characteristic of the schools of Swinburne in England and Baudelaire in France. In prose Poe wrote able but partisan literary criti-

cisms, and weird tales which are inferior only to those of Hawthorne. He was born in 1811, and died in 1849.

20. OTHER POETS. — American literature has been uncommonly fertile in poets who, though they have not reached the first rank, have written well and proved their right to the name. James Gates Percival, a melancholy and shy scholar, wrote *A Dream of a Day*, and other pieces which have retained popularity for their sentiment and smooth versification. N. P. Willis and George P. Morris, long associated on a New York family journal, were poets whose reputation has not been a lasting one. Willis wrote scriptural pieces of much power, and his present neglect by the public is as unjust as its previous flattery was unwise. The artificiality of his poems has been their ruin. Morris wrote spirited and popular songs, which are still sung. Edward Coate Pinkney, of Baltimore, was the author of lyrics which Poe insisted would have made him famous had he lived in New England. Charles Fenno Hoffman, still living, but long incurably insane, was also a facile lyrist, and wrote a novel and books of travel. George H. Calvert has produced many dramas and poems, but his biographies of Goethe and Rubens are better worth preservation. Dr. Thomas Dunn English became famous by a single song, *Ben Bolt;* he has since devoted himself more particularly to national poems. George H. Boker, of Philadelphia, has

zealously tried to better the condition of the meagre field of American dramatic literature; and some of his plays have strength and fire. Charles T. Brooks has made a good translation of the first part of *Faust*, and has rendered many of the most famous German lyrics into English. C. P. Cranch's translation of the *Æneid* of Virgil, in unrhymed pentameter, ranks with the other books in the recent notable series of American translations. Mr. Cranch has also put into original poetry a painter's color and art. The *Divine Comedy* of Dante has been partially translated by Dr. T. W. Parsons, of Boston, at the expense of his original verse, which is of excellent quality. Alfred B. Street's numerous poems are mainly devoted to the celebration of nature. W. W. Story, once a neighbor and friend of Lowell's but latterly a resident of Rome, has joined poetry and sculpture, just as Allston and Cranch have united poetry and painting, and with equal success. Notwithstanding the multiplicity of religious denominations in this country, few good hymns have been written during the present century. As far as literature goes, our humor has been better than our piety. The greatest development of American humor, in prose and verse, has been of late years, but before the war John G. Saxe had become famous for his clever travesties, puns, and love poems. As a poet of pure merriment he is unsurpassed. The first of a numerous body of social satires was William Allen Butler's *Nothing to Wear*, published in 1857. Not until recently have we had any female poets of the first rank; those writing before the war, save the Cary sisters, Alice and Phœbe, having been almost without exception slaves of the sentimentality which Mrs. Hemans and L. E. L. had made fashionable in England.

21. ORATORS. — During the present century, certainly in its first half, oratory has equaled its splendid beginning a hundred years ago. Unquestionably, the speeches of Daniel Webster, John C. Calhoun, Henry Clay, Edward Everett, Rufus Choate, William H. Seward, Charles Sumner, Robert C. Winthrop, William Lloyd Garrison, and Wendell Phillips belong to literature. Fortunately, the principal orations and addresses of all of them have been well edited and issued in suitable form for preservation and study, being in many cases revised by the authors themselves.

22. HISTORIANS. — At first sight the number of notable American historians seems small; but a comparison with other nations shows that during the present century we have had more than our share of historical writers of the first rank. Where libraries have not been accessible, our industrious investigators have created them; and their zeal and accuracy have made foreign countries their debtors, conspicuously in the case of Prescott, Motley, and Parkman.

23. RICHARD HILDRETH was born in Deerfield, Massachusetts, in 1807, and died in Florence, Italy, in 1865. He graduated at Harvard in 1826, studied law, and then entered journalism. Like Motley, Hildreth began his literary career by writing a feeble novel, called *Archy Moore* (1837), directed against slavery, whose evils the author, like Channing, had beheld while on a tour for his health. Afterwards he wrote, in books and in the newspapers, in favor of free banking and against Texan annexation. Another forgotten work of his was a campaign life of Harrison; and Hildreth also took a lively share in the theological controversies at that time still smouldering in Boston. A *Theory of Morals* and *Theory of Politics* were written while the author was editing a paper in British Guiana. A longer list of obscure works written by a famous author need not be asked for; but Hildreth stepped to the front rank in his *History of the United States*, which he had been planning to write all his life, and for which plenty of material had been accumulated. It begins with the discovery of America, and ends with the first presidential term of James Monroe. Its style is rather dry.

24. GEORGE BANCROFT, the author of the other chief history of the United States, was also born in Massachusetts and graduated at Harvard. His studies were completed at Göttingen, then the fashionable German university for American students,

and on his return he published a volume of poems and a translation of a work on ancient Greece. An attempt to found an American Eton at Northampton, Massachusetts, in which Bancroft took part, was soon abandoned. The first volume of his *History of the United States*, the standard work on the subject, both for its matter and manner, appeared in 1834. Since that time he has toiled diligently and pretty constantly upon it, though the tenth volume did not appear until 1874, the author having meanwhile been secretary of the navy and minister to England and Prussia. The style of the work is brilliant, and the author excels in descriptive passages. His frank comments on the characters mentioned have brought down upon him a shower of pamphlets written by descendants or partisans of the officers criticised. The work begins with Columbus and ends in 1782. A revised edition was prepared by the author in 1876.

25. JOHN GORHAM PALFREY, another Massachusetts man and Harvard graduate, who for the first fifty years of his life was a student of biblical literature and a politician, in both of which characters he was successful, began in 1858 a *History of New England*, which, with no great charm of language, holds a high rank for completeness and accuracy. No other part of the country has found so full a historian. Four volumes had been issued previous to 1878.

26. WILLIAM HICKLING PRESCOTT, the most brilliant and famous of American historians, was a descendant of William Prescott, who fought at Bunker Hill. While at Harvard, in 1812, his left eye was so injured that during the rest of his life Prescott was partly blind, and had to employ an amanuensis and a mechanical contrivance for writing. Luckily, his means were ample and he was able to pursue his studies, in the midst of a remarkable literary coterie, until he was thirty years old, when he determined to write his *History of Ferdinand and Isabella*. The composition of the work occupied him eleven years, and the author expended much money in the accumulation of material. It was immediately translated into five European languages, and became the most celebrated work of history written on this side of the Atlantic. Prescott's *Conquest of Mexico* (1843), *Conquest of Peru* (1847), and *Philip the Second* (1855–1858), were not less successful. He also edited Robertson's *Charles V.*, and collected from the reviews a volume of *Miscellanies*. Three more volumes of *Philip the Second* were planned. Prescott died in Boston in 1859, and his life was written by his friend George Ticknor. Not since Milton has so high a reputation been won by a man practically blind; and no historian in the language has written in a more graceful and eloquent style.

27. JOHN LOTHROP MOTLEY was born in 1814,

studied at Harvard and Göttingen, wrote a novel in early life, and in 1856 published *The Rise of the Dutch Republic*, which has attracted readers and translators only fewer than Prescott's. Less ornate than Prescott, Motley is not less readable, and as a political analyst he is unexcelled. *The History of the United Netherlands* was published between 1861 and 1868, and the *Life of John of Barneveld* in 1874. Motley, like Irving, Bancroft, Lowell, Marsh, Boker, and Howells, represented the United States abroad. He died in 1877.

28. OTHER HISTORIANS. — Jared Sparks, president of Harvard between 1849 and 1852, wrote many biographies and theological works, and brought out between 1834 and 1837, in twelve massive volumes, Washington's writings, together with a life. In 1840 he finished a similar edition of Franklin, in ten volumes. Both works are indispensable, as is Dr. Sparks's *Diplomatic Correspondence of the American Revolution* (1830). Francis Parkman, like Prescott partially blind, is publishing a great work with the general title of *France and England in North America*, of which five parts had appeared in 1878. His style is singularly graceful, and he is the most readable of American historians save Prescott and Motley. John Foster Kirk, Prescott's private secretary, has prepared a good and standard history of *Charles the Bold*, issued between 1863 and 1867. Richard Frothing-

ham has written a complete monograph on the siege of Boston. Samuel Eliot, formerly president of Trinity College, is the author of an elaborate *History of Liberty*. A great library of serviceable popular histories by the brothers Jacob and John S. C. Abbott were justly honored by President Lincoln's remark that he had derived from them all his knowledge of history. The larger works of John S. C. Abbott are injured by their partisan tone, though they are very readable. George W. Greene's *Historical View of the American Revolution* is the best condensed record of the time, and excels in its analysis of causes of events. His life of his grandfather, General Nathanael Greene, was called out in response to Bancroft's strictures. Parke Godwin published in 1860 the first volume of a history of France, never since continued.

29. TRAVELERS. — As next of kin to historians, mention should be made of a few travelers, though in this department we have less to boast of: Elisha Kent Kane, Charles F. Hall, and Isaac I. Hayes in the Arctic region; John Ross Browne, Thomas W. Knox, and Commodore Charles Wilkes in voyages around the world; E. G. Squier and J. L. Stephens in Central America; Eugene Schuyler in Turkistan; and Frederick Law Olmsted in the Southern States. Benson J. Lossing's *Field-book of the Revolution* is both travel and history.

30. FICTION. — JAMES FENIMORE COOPER. — Charles Brockden Brown began the long line of American novels, but James Fenimore Cooper was the first writer of fiction to be extensively read. Born in Burlington, New Jersey, in 1789, he spent his boyhood at Cooperstown, Otsego County, New York, a village founded by his father in 1786. Having studied three years at Yale, he entered the navy as midshipman in 1805, remaining in the service six years, and acquiring that knowledge of the sea which he afterwards put to such good use in his books. *Precaution*, his first novel, was published anonymously in 1821. It met with no great success, being a tame story of the English type, though subsequently Cooper's readers gave it a higher place in their esteem. *The Spy* (1821) found a multitude of admirers, and was republished in Europe in many translations. This story, as well as *The Pioneers*, issued the next year, was thoroughly national, and Cooper thenceforward occupied as his own the field of wild life in the West. His novels were full of romantic interest, and showed the public that American scenery and life furnished as good a foundation for fiction as the castles of Europe. *The Last of the Mohicans* (1826) is one of the best of the remarkable group of stories called the Leatherstocking Tales. Cooper was American through and through. He did not hesitate in some of his later stories to

satirize the "louder" national characteristics; but to him more than any other author is due the increasing attention to home subjects and heroes. From his writings, undoubtedly, a part of the English public got the impression, which it has with difficulty corrected, that buffaloes and Indians form the most conspicuous features in our civilization. Half of Cooper's better works were devoted to the sea, the most successful being *The Pilot* (1823) and *The Red Rover* (1827). Cooper's quarrels with his countrymen were numerous, chiefly because he thought them lukewarm in national pride; and he increased the hostility of the newspaper press by a multitude of libel suits, in many of which he was successful. *The Pathfinder* and *The Deerslayer* appeared in 1840 and 1841; and *Afloat and Ashore* three years later. An elaborate *Naval History of the United States* and a series of biographies of naval officers were among the other writings of this industrious author, who by no means confined himself to a single field. His last book was *The Ways of the Hour*, an attack on the system of trial by jury, in the form of a story, somewhat in the style later adopted by Charles Reade. Cooper's novels have won high praise from the first critical authorities, including Bryant and Prescott, but his later books, with no diminution of merit, found fewer readers than their predecessors. Cooper virtually had the field to himself, at first, and the novelty of his subjects aroused in his writings an interest which their intrinsic literary merits hardly warranted. In later years a host of imitators have written more exaggerated Indian stories, which long formed the principal literary diet of the lower classes, though their popularity is now somewhat waning.

31. NATHANIEL HAWTHORNE, whom James Russell Lowell has called the greatest imaginative writer since Shakespeare, was born in Salem in 1804, of an old colonial family, some of whose members, as a matter of conviction, had taken part in the persecutions which made the early history of that town so famous. In later years the Hawthornes (who spelled their name Hathorne) had followed the sea, and Nathaniel's father, a shipmaster, died at Surinam in 1808. From his mother the boy inherited a morbid disposition, that lady having so grieved over her husband's loss that for thirty years she insisted on isolating herself in her room. Nathaniel was a feeble child, but was able to enter Bowdoin College at seventeen, where, as has been seen, Longfellow was his classmate. His intimate friend, however, was Franklin Pierce, a member of the class next above him. On graduation he returned to Salem, and outdid his mother in absolute seclusion, writing all day, and stalking over the ancient town at night. *Fanshawe*, an anonymous romance, was published in Boston in 1828, but was never acknowledged by the author.

For years it was a great literary curiosity, but has lately been reprinted. It is a somewhat crude production, but full of the power which afterwards made the author famous. In 1836 Hawthorne became the editor of the *American Magazine of Useful Knowledge,* published in Boston; of which, though nominally editor, Hawthorne was, in fact, the sole author. He had destroyed many of his earlier pieces, but by 1837 he was able to collect enough stories to form the *Twice Told Tales.* Longfellow and other critics saw and said what they were, but the general public failed to appreciate them. The first edition contained only half the present work, and a revision, with a second series, appeared in 1842, and found a few more readers. Bancroft, who was then collector of the port of Boston, gave Hawthorne a place in the custom-house in that city, which he lost on the accession of Harrison in 1841. A short sojourn at the famous Brook Farm in West Roxbury followed; and everywhere the shy, mysterious romancer was the shrewdest and minutest of observers. In 1843 he took up his abode in the old Ripley house at Concord, close by the bridge where the "embattled farmers stood." Hawthorne's residence in old houses was partly from accident and partly from choice; but of all his homes this was most to his liking, and in the volumes called *Mosses from an Old Manse* (1846) he has celebrated it in the choicest language. This collection of stories and sketches was in the same general style as the *Twice Told Tales*. Emerson had been a former occupant of the house, and Hawthorne's Concord neighbors were Emerson, Thoreau, and the younger Ellery Channing. In 1846 Hawthorne became surveyor at the Salem custom-house, and, as usual, made his residence there an opportunity for the industrious collection of literary material. The advent of the Whigs into power, for the second time, once more displaced him, and he retired to a little cottage in Lenox, Massachusetts, having published in 1850 *The Scarlet Letter*, a very powerful and dramatic colonial romance, written in faultless English. At Lenox Hawthorne was unusually industrious, writing in 1851 *The House of the Seven Gables*, embodying his Salem sight-seeings, — a story still more intense and solemn than any of its predecessors. *The Blithedale Romance* (1852) was founded on his Brook Farm experiences, and combined the loftiest humor with the deepest pathos. Zenobia, the heroine, is probably the greatest of Hawthorne's creations. The same year, 1852, Hawthorne wrote a third series of *Twice Told Tales*, and a campaign life of Pierce, for whom, ever since his college days, he had maintained a strong friendship. Hawthorne's firm adherence to Democratic opinions was singular, for he was the last man in the country whom one would have suspected of any political interest whatever. Thoreau was not more unworldly, and yet Hawthorne constantly endeavored to help his party in every way. There was no suspicion of time-serving, and when, in 1853, the romancer was given the Liverpool consulate, both parties rejoiced. For the first time in his life Hawthorne was in easy circumstances, though a thriftier man would have made more money out of his lucrative position. Resigning in 1857, he spent three years in England, France, and Italy. His *English* and *Italian Note-Books*, published posthumously, are full of these experiences of one of the best of sight-seers. The *American Note-Books* consist of his home diaries, and contain hints for a hundred books, which none but Hawthorne ever could write. *Our Old Home*, sights and scenes in England, was published in 1863, during the author's life-time. *The Marble Faun* appeared in 1860, — an Italian romance, by some considered his best work. Hawthorne had brought out three juvenile books between 1851 and 1853, — being stories of history and mythology; and after his death were found a fragment of *The Dolliver Romance* and *Septimius Felton*, a strange story of the soul. So ends the list of the works of the foremost American prose writer.

32. OTHER NOVELISTS. — Robert Montgomery Bird, a Philadelphia physician, wrote Mexican historical romances, and *Nick of the Woods*, a story of

Kentucky in the Revolution. John Neal, one of the most long-lived and voluminous of our writers, was the author of several American tales. Another historical novelist was William Ware, a Unitarian clergyman, whose *Aurelian, Julian,* and *Zenobia,* illustrated life in ancient Rome. Sylvester Judd, also a Unitarian minister, wrote in 1845 *Margaret: a tale of the Real and the Ideal;* which has by some been considered the greatest of our works of fiction, while others find its whims and crotchets so numerous as to make it almost unreadable. This work was illustrated by Darley in a remarkable series of outline designs. William Gilmore Simms, one of the leading Southern writers of the century, was born in 1806 and died in 1870. He wrote many poems, but is chiefly remembered by his novels, among which are *The Yemassee, The Partisan,* and *Beauchampe.* John Esten Cooke, of Virginia, has written less, but his novels of Southern life are equally meritorious. The best of them is *The Virginia Comedians,* an admirable picture of the courtly Virginian of the elder day. Charles F. Briggs, a native of Nantucket and all his life a journalist in New York, wrote contemporary novels pleasantly combining satire and humor; *Harry Franco* in 1839, and *The Haunted Merchant* in 1843. Richard B. Kimball has also illustrated in fiction the every-day life of New York city. Dr. William Starbuck Mayo, in *Never Again,* has likewise held the mirror up to modern American society. John P. Kennedy, secretary of the navy under Fillmore, wrote good novels of old-time society, in his *Swallow Barn* and *Horse-Shoe Robinson*. Herman Melville has written lively sea tales. Thus our indigenous fiction presents a good showing. Of female writers the number is of late years greatly increasing. Harriet Beecher Stowe's *Uncle Tom's Cabin* (1852), a novel directed against slavery, has had the greatest popular success of any American book, having sold between five and six hundred thousand copies in this country alone, and having been forty times translated. Her later novels, though superior from a literary point of view, have naturally appealed to a more limited interest. *The Minister's Wooing* and *The Pearl of Orr's Island* are faithful New England pictures, and *Oldtown Folks,* one of her later books, introduces her best creation, Sam Lawson. Next to *Uncle Tom,* as a literary success, came *The Wide, Wide World* of the sisters Susan and Anna Warner, published in 1850. Other popular female novelists have been Catherine M. Sedgwick, the author of *Hope Leslie;* Miriam Coles Harris, who wrote *Rutledge;* and Maria S. Cummins, whose *Lamplighter* is one of the best of American novels. "Grace Greenwood" (Sara J. Lippincott) and "Fanny Fern" (Mrs. James Parton) have written sketches and stories of interest, though mostly ephemeral in value.

33. EMERSON AND THE CONCORD AUTHORS. — Ralph Waldo Emerson is the most distinguished of American essayists, and his influence on thought and style has been marked for forty years, making Concord our literary Mecca. The descendant of eight generations of clergymen, Emerson was born in Boston in 1803, and graduated at Harvard in 1821. Between 1829 and 1832 he was a Unitarian minister, but left the pulpit in consequence of his radical opinions. Having made a short trip to Europe, he began his career as a lecturer, in which capacity he has become more famous than any other American author. A slender book on *Nature* made a great stir among thoughtful people in 1839. In 1838 he had delivered his celebrated address before the divinity school at Cambridge, and his personal influence became very great in forming the "Transcendental" movement, an attempt to abandon traditional forms and society's chains and to get back to nature's freedom of thought and rectitude of action. *The Dial* was the organ of the school in 1840, and Margaret Fuller, Emerson, Alcott, Thoreau, and the younger Channing wrote for it. Emerson's two series of *Essays* appeared in 1841 and 1844; *Representative Men*, a course of lectures, in 1850; *English Traits* in 1856; *The Conduct of Life* in 1860; *Society and Solitude* in 1870; and *Letters and Social Aims* in 1876; in which year a carefully revised edition of his poems was also published. Emerson's

style is highly finished, notwithstanding the fact that his essays are often like the random leaves of many years' study. His influence is as spontaneous as that of nature; he announces, and lets others plead. Henry D. Thoreau was a recluse who long lived on the shores of Walden Pond, in Concord, providing for his simple wants by hunting and gardening. *Walden* is his best book; but in six other volumes he carries the reader straight to Nature's heart. Amos Bronson Alcott, at first an educator, has been the sole representative in this country of the art of imparting knowledge by "conversations," which he has held for many years in various parts of the United States, though residing in Concord. Of latter years he has collected some of his writings into books, the essays being even more condensed than Emerson's. William Ellery Channing, a nephew of the famous divine, has written a biography of Thoreau and a volume of poems.

34. MISCELLANEOUS WRITERS. — George William Curtis, whose style entitles him to be called the American Charles Lamb, has written a great number of essays in periodicals; three graceful books of Eastern travel; *The Potiphar Papers*, the best social satire produced in this country; and *Trumps*, a readable novel. George Ticknor, professor of modern languages at Harvard between 1817 and 1835, produced in 1849 an elaborate *History of Spanish Literature*, twice since revised, and

accepted here and abroad as the standard. Edwin P. Whipple is the most faithful of American critics, and in his several volumes has given a thorough review of many of the best English and American books, — his researches in Elizabethan literature being his chief work. George S. Hillard wrote in 1853 a good account of travel in Italy; and another book of Italian thought and experience, somewhat more artistic, was published by Charles Eliot Norton in 1859. The *Two Years Before the Mast* of Richard H. Dana, Jr., a record of personal experience, is the American classic of travel. In books of local observation and experience, the White Mountains have been well described by Thomas Starr King; and the peculiar life of Cape Cod in the stories of Charles Nordhoff. The *Letters from New York* of Mrs. Lydia Maria Child made a sensation in their day. Mrs. Child's *Progress of Religious Ideas* (1855) and *Aspirations of the World* (1878) are valuable contributions to the study of the science of religion. Her *Appeal in behalf of that Class of Americans called Africans* (1832) is noteworthy as the first contribution of a woman to the antislavery literature of the country. It was an admirable little work, and helped to carry Wendell Phillips into the antislavery movement. Joseph C. Neal's *Charcoal Sketches* and George H. Derby's *Phœnixiana* were the predecessors of the later flock of humorous books. F. S. Cozzens pleasantly described the Nova Scotians. The brothers Henry and William B. Reed wrote literary and historical criticisms. Samuel G. Goodrich put history and natural history into popular forms, and wrote in readable fashion on all sorts of subjects. H. W. Herbert first dignified field sports by making them the subject of well-written books. Donald G. Mitchell wrote *Dream-Life* and *The Reveries of a Bachelor*, which have never lost a strong hold on popularity; and he has also treated farm subjects pleasantly, and is the author of *Dr. Johns*, a successful novel. Dr. Edward Robinson, in his *Biblical Researches*, published between 1841 and 1856, produced a work which is considered a standard in all countries. He was the father of biblical archæology in America. Several standard editions of Shakespeare have been edited in this country, chief among them being those of Richard Grant White and Horace Howard Furness. Delia Bacon and Nathaniel Holmes have supported the theory that Lord Bacon wrote the plays. Dr. J. G. Holland is a sensible and plain-spoken popular essayist, and has written excellent novels of American life, — *Miss Gilbert's Career*, *Arthur Bonnicastle*, and *The Story of Sevenoaks* being the best of them. As a poet he has been equally popular, though with less deserts. Henry T. Tuckerman, in numerous books and a host of essays, did good service to native literature and art.

35. SCIENTIFIC AND SPECIAL WRITERS. — In law and medicine the number of American books is of course large, but none save the *Commentaries on American Law* of James Kent and the *International Law* of Henry Wheaton — both classics — need be mentioned here; nor can the many writers on science be specified, whose works are for the most part connected with literature by a slender thread. The dictionaries of Noah Webster and Joseph E. Worcester; the philological works of William D. Whitney, George P. Marsh, Francis J. Child, S. S. Haldeman, E. A. Sophocles, F. A. March, and James Hadley; the botanical writings of John Torrey and Asa Gray; the mathematical and astronomical publications of Nathaniel Bowditch, Elias Loomis, Benjamin Peirce, and Simon Newcomb; the ethnological works of H. R. Schoolcraft, H. H. Bancroft, and C. C. Jones, Jr.; the books on birds by J. J. Audubon, Elliott Coues, and T. M. Brewer; the geological treatises of Louis Agassiz, Edward Hitchcock, and James D. Dana; and the physical geographies of Arnold Guyot, are some of the best of our contributions to knowledge. W. J. Hardee, Winfield Scott, H. W. Halleck, and George B. McClellan have published books on military science. In political economy Henry C. Carey has strongly favored protection; and Dr. Theodore D. Woolsey, formerly president of Yale, has long been an authority on international law and political science.

CHAPTER IV.

AFTER 1861.

1. LITERATURE OF THE CIVIL WAR. — It is still convenient to follow the division of time by wars, omitting that with Mexico, which formed no break in current history. As in the Revolution and the War of 1812, very little that was notable was added to the literature of the country by the civil war of 1861. Most of the poets wrote one or two stirring pieces, and many new writers came into notice by the publication of meritorious occasional verse. But as a rule the creative powers of our best authors seemed somewhat benumbed, though, strangely enough, books and readers greatly multiplied between 1861 and 1864, partly in consequence of the largely increased circulation of the periodical press. Immediately on the close of the struggle, and even during its progress, many popular histories were hurried upon the market, but of course the events described were yet too fresh in mind to permit impartiality on either side. A vast *Rebellion Record*, edited by Frank Moore, has preserved plenty of material for the future writer. This useful work is arranged under three divisions;

a diary of events, a reissue of leading documents of importance, and a liberal selection from popular poetry and newspaper incidents on both sides. Of the histories that have thus far appeared, those by Horace Greeley and Alexander H. Stephens are fullest in their accounts of the antislavery contest which preceded and attended the war; while that by Dr. John W. Draper, a student of politics and science, is the nearest approach yet made to an unpartisan record. The first volume of Mr. Greeley's history (which is comprised in two) is more valuable than the second, for in it a life-long spectator and combatant in the antislavery struggle records the events with which he was so closely connected. Mr. Stephens's work lays great stress upon the rise and development of the doctrine of state rights, of which the author is an able defender. Elaborate as is Mr. Greeley's story of the slavery agitation, a still larger and more valuable history thereof is contained in Vice-President Wilson's *Rise and Fall of the Slave Power in America*, comprised in three volumes. Mr. Wilson's knowledge of political history was as extensive as Mr. Greeley's, and the judicial quality of his mind somewhat more marked. He had the advantage, furthermore, of writing long after the close of the war, instead of in its midst. This history was the closing, and in some sense the most valuable, work of his life. Many of the generals engaged on either side have published their reminiscences of campaigns, at greater or less length. Of these, General Sherman's were at once the most important and outspoken, and called out many replies from injured officers. Lieutenant-General Scott published in 1864 two volumes of autobiography, having a somewhat modest literary and historical value.

2. POETS. — Of recent years American poetry has been somewhat influenced by the English pre-Raphaelites, whose methods and tastes Poe, to a certain extent, had foreshadowed twenty years before. A renewed interest in purely national or local subjects, in this country, accompanied, rather than was caused by, the new-romanticism of the English writers of the Swinburne school, who have found in our Whitman and Miller greater merits to admire than in the more conventional writers whom the majority of readers are accustomed to revere. Their celebration of the wilder elements in our life, and their freedom from restraint, have seemed admirable to London-bred critics; and their English friends have doubtless taken pleasure in singling out for special praise writers whose clientage was not so numerous in this country, and whose subjects would seem stranger in London than in New York. The old inattention to our literature, on the part of Englishmen, has given place to a somewhat injudicious and undiscriminating praise. But, fostered by home development and foreign admira-

tion, an original and excellent element in American literature has rapidly grown within the past twelve years. The great majority of our writers, however, have been content to work faithfully in the old paths, and many living authors, popularly assigned to the second rank, may fairly be called the peers of some of their predecessors of higher reputation.

3. BAYARD TAYLOR had acquired a substantial literary reputation before the date at which this chapter begins ; but since his future renown will chiefly rest, doubtless, upon his volumes of poems published since 1862, it is well to enter his name in this place. He was born at Kennett Square, a Pennsylvania country town, in 1825, and while a very young man became famous for a vivacious account of a pedestrian tour in Europe. California, Egypt, Asia Minor, India, Japan, and other countries were afterwards visited by the indefatigable tourist, whose numerous books of travel proved to have great popular interest, and permanent value for reference. In 1863 Mr. Taylor published his first novel, *Hannah Thurston*, which was followed within the next seven years by *John Godfrey's Fortunes*, *The Story of Kennett*, and *Joseph and his Friend*. These four novels, besides ingeniousness of plot and cleverness of situation, are noted for their accurate pictures of American life, especially in the Quaker region of Pennsylvania, which the author knows thoroughly.

Between 1844 and 1855 Mr. Taylor put forth seven volumes of poetry, chiefly noteworthy for lyrical excellence. *The Poet's Journal* (1862), *The Picture of St. John* (1866), *The Masque of the Gods* (1872), *Lars* (1873), and *The Prophet* (1874), a Mormon drama, are more elaborate works. In lyrical facility Mr. Taylor may fairly be said to surpass almost any living writer save Swinburne ; and as a dramatist he has fire and force. Some of his longer poems have been produced with a rapidity recalling the Italian *improvisatori*. *The Echo Club* (published in 1876, though written in 1872) is a series of clever imitations of the leading poets of the century. A translation of both parts of *Faust* appeared in 1870 and 1871, in which the original metres were reproduced with surprising faithfulness.

4. RICHARD HENRY STODDARD, a native of Hingham, Massachusetts, is the author of nine volumes of short poems, full of the genius of the true poet, and written in a style of which high finish is the chief mark. He has been an editor of many collections of verse, and of several volumes of literary reminiscence.

5. JOHN GODFREY SAXE, born in Vermont in 1816, has been more successful than any other American poet in classical travesties and in witty turns of language. His collected poems do not fill a large volume, but are full of airiness and grace. As a sonneteer Mr. Saxe has won a high place. His

humorous poems with a moral are neatly pointed, and his fables and legends are equally happy, whether their subjects are old or new.

6. JOHN TOWNSEND TROWBRIDGE, born in 1827, first became known as a writer of excellent juvenile stories signed by Paul Creyton. *Father Brighthopes* and *The Old Battle-Ground* are the best of them. *Neighbor Jackwood* (1857) has hardly been surpassed as a picture of American home life in the country. Mr. Trowbridge's other novels are *Cudjo's Cave*, *The Three Scouts*, *Lucy Arlyn*, and *Neighbor's Wives*. The two first dealt with the civil war, during which they were very popular. Upon his poems, though few in number, Mr. Trowbridge has expended his greatest care. *The Vagabonds* (1864) is an excellent union of pathos and humor; in his lesser lyrics and in the five poems grouped under the title of *The Book of Gold* (1877) subjects of love, or life, or humor are handled in pleasing fashion.

7. WALT WHITMAN was born at West Hills, Long Island, in 1819, and began life as a school-teacher and literary man, writing rather feeble stories and indifferent poems for the magazines, in the ordinary style, under the name of Walter Whitman. In 1855, reducing Walter to Walt, he printed in Brooklyn a peculiar volume called *Leaves of Grass*, — rhapsody rather than poetry, being neither rhymed nor versified. This work, which has several times been enlarged, is devoted to a large variety of subjects,

many of the poems being personal, while all are pervaded with a love of liberty in conscience and politics. The catalogue style is a prevailing blemish, and Whitman's overruling desire to be natural makes him fall into real affectations; but there are many strong and fine lines in the poems. *O Captain, my Captain*, shows that he is not fettered by rhyme. *When Lilacs last in the Dooryard bloomed* is the best poem evoked by the assassination of President Lincoln.

8. JOAQUIN MILLER, whose real name is Cincinnatus Heine Miller, has been miner, Nicaraguan, Indian resident, and county judge. *Songs of the Sierras*, wild poems of the West, somewhat polished in versification by a careful study and thorough admiration of Byron and Swinburne, appeared in London in 1870. *Songs of the Sunlands* and *The Ship in the Desert* are later poems, and the author has written an Italian novel, an account of life among the Indians, a collection of graphic prose sketches of life in the far West, called *The First Fam'lies of the Sierras*, and a society story in verse, *The Baroness of New York*. Miller is a sort of Oregon Byron in his freedom of spirit and his love of rhythmical luxuriance, and he has cultivated with success a wholly original field in literature. Old-world subjects, however, are equally fresh in his hands. Whitman and Miller are the chief American kindred of the English pre-Raphaelites, but

their kinship is one of nature and not of imitation. None of our other coadjutors of Rossetti and Swinburne deserve mention save Edgar Fawcett, whose poetical descriptions of flowers and animals are uncommonly happy; and Adah Isaacs Menken, who wrote gloomily pathetic verse in Whitman's unrhymed and unmetrical style.

9. FRANCIS BRET HARTE, a native of Albany, has written short stories and sketches of California life, having wonderful wit and pathos, of which *The Luck of Roaring Camp* and *The Outcasts of Poker Flat* are the best. Of his poems some are in dialect, *The Heathen Chinee* having had the widest circulation of any recent poem. The author has written a long novel, *Gabriel Conroy;* and *Thankful Blossom*, a novelette of Revolutionary times in New Jersey. *Two Men of Sandy Bar*, a drama, is a stage presentation of some of the characters of the mining region, including a curious export to California, Colonel Culpepper Starbottle. The singular beauty of Mr. Harte's society poems, which are witty and graceful, has not been ignored by the public in consequence of the greater success of his more characteristic productions. His *Condensed Novels*, prose burlesques several times revised, are better than Thackeray's.

10. JOHN HAY. — The popular dialect poetry of the time finds its best illustration in the *Jim Bludso* of John Hay, a native of Indiana, who

was President Lincoln's secretary during the war. A volume called *Pike County Ballads* includes this poem and others as good. Mr. Hay was the originator of a fashion in which he found a troop of imitators but no equals, owing to his slow method of composition and his faithful literary artisanship. The same honesty appears in a very different form in *Castilian Days*, a prose volume of finished Spanish sketches. Other original writers of dialect verse have been Charles Godfrey Leland, who in various *Hans Breitmann* volumes put the veritable Pennsylvania Dutchman into amusing verse; Charles G. Halpine, whose Miles O'Reilly was a favorite Hibernian figure during the war; and W. M. Carleton, who, without the aid of misspelling, has celebrated the average Western farmer and his wife.

11. THOMAS BAILEY ALDRICH is one of the many natives of Portsmouth, New Hampshire, who have won success in literature. His boyhood was passed in that ancient seaport town, in New Orleans, and in New York. Before he was twenty he became an industrious worker on the New York press, and his first book was published when he was but nineteen. *The Ballad of Babie Bell* (afterwards entitled *Baby Bell*), a faultless poem of child-death, has had for twenty years a permanent place in popular favor. Between 1855 and 1862 Mr. Aldrich published several small volumes of poems, a pretty little juvenile story in prose, and *Out of His Head*,

a curious romance never reissued by the author. In 1865 Mr. Aldrich collected his complete poetical works in a single volume. He has always been his own severest critic, and has sternly rejected poems the public would prefer to keep, besides revising others which seemed excellent at first. This collected edition was again carefully revised ten years later, and put forth under the title of *Cloth of Gold*. *Flower and Thorn* (1876) comprises all the additional poems which the author cares to preserve. Mr. Aldrich's genius is of a rare and delicate quality; his power of expression is graceful; and his care in composition is such that he writes nothing perishable. His lyrics are full of melody, and his few sonnets are among the best written by American poets. *Friar Jerome's Beautiful Book* and *Garnaut Hall*, longer pieces in blank verse, are in a narrative style which the author has seldom cultivated. After a considerable pause, Mr. Aldrich began to write prose once more, in the form of short stories and sketches, having an exquisite humor, and chiefly notable for surprising cleverness of situation. *The Story of a Bad Boy* (1869), his second juvenile, reproduced in its Tom Bailey the author's youthful experiences in Portsmouth, which, as "Rivermouth," appears in nearly all his stories. *Prudence Palfrey* (1874) and *The Queen of Sheba* (1877) are novels of moderate length, having, in substance, the finish and quiet humor of the shorter stories.

12. EDMUND CLARENCE STEDMAN is likewise eminent as a lyrist. A member of the Yale class of 1853, he has for the most of his life been a banker, though writing constantly for the press. *The Diamond Wedding* (1859) first attracted general attention as a brilliant social satire, though the author was already doing better work in shorter poems. *Alice of Monmouth*, a war story in verse, succeeded *Poems, Lyric and Idyllic*. *The Blameless Prince* was Mr. Stedman's third volume. These three books, though each beginning with a long poem, were chiefly excellent for purely lyrical beauty. In 1873 a collected edition appeared. Of its contents the poems called *The Doorstep, Toujours Amour*, and *Laura, my Darling* (to his wife) have been most liked, and have found a permanent place in the anthologies. *Hawthorne, and Other Poems* (1877), a thin volume, includes the later pieces, the first being the finest tribute yet paid to the memory of the romancer. In his *Victorian Poets* (1876) is presented an elaborate review of the entire body of contemporary English verse. It is the most careful and judicial of American books of criticism, and is especially just toward the new-romantic school, with the works of the humblest members of which Mr. Stedman is intimately acquainted. It is written in a style so polished that it seems artificial to the hasty reader.

13. THE PIATTS, John James and his wife Sallie

M. Bryan, have written no long pieces, but have been, in a sense true of very few other American authors, "poets' poets." Mrs. Piatt's conceits and moods are more marked than those of her husband, but in her poems pathos and sentiment are real. Her subjects are novel and their elaboration delicate. Mr. Piatt's condensation of style never becomes obscure, and he is happy in his descriptions of natural scenery.

14. OTHER POETS. — In the Southern newspapers, during the civil war, there was a considerable amount of war poetry, the best of which was written by Henry Timrod, whose *Spring* is his finest poem. Paul H. Hayne, of Georgia, is unsurpassed as a sonneteer, and his poetry catches the spirit of Southern scenery. He is also successful in depicting the scenes and portraying the character of mediævalism. Of northern poets made famous by their war poems, the chief not hitherto mentioned are Henry Howard Brownell, who wrote spirited naval pieces; Forceythe Willson, the author of *The Old Sergeant* and of non-martial poems of still greater excellence; Elbridge J. Cutler, a Harvard professor, whose ringing and finished *War Lyrics*, though admirable, he modestly printed in the smallest of editions; and Thomas Buchanan Read, who found in his *Sheridan's Ride* a popularity never won by his previous poems. Mrs. Julia Ward Howe's *Battle Hymn of the Republic* was more

famous during the struggle than any other single lyric. Of non-martial poets, William Winter, one of the greatest favorites in a knot of brilliant young journalists living in New York about 1861, has written several small volumes of verse, graceful and tender, and pervaded with a constant sense of sadness. George Arnold was another member of this coterie of newspaper men. He had some elements of permanent success in his delicacy of rhythm and gloomy, but not morbid, depth of feeling. Richard Watson Gilder's *New Day* is an American outgrowth of the early Italian school of poetry. George P. Lathrop's *Rose and Roof-Tree* includes pieces which, while thoroughly original, are half Tennysonian in their treatment of landscape. Sidney Lanier wrote in 1876 a curious *Centennial Ode to Columbia*, which aims to be in poetry some such thing as Wagner's music is in orchestration. Of recent female poets of high rank the number is surprisingly large, and half the poems in current periodicals are by women. As a rule they write short poems of mood or description, rather than of creation or narration. Margaret J. Preston, Elizabeth Akers Allen, Rose Terry Cooke, Nora Perry, Lucy Larcom, Celia Thaxter, and Helen Fiske Jackson (" H. H.") are the most eminent. Mrs. Thaxter's poems of the sea are the fruit of long acquaintance with the barren Isles of Shoals in New Hampshire. Mrs. Jackson's prose sketches in *Bits of Travel* and *Bits of Talk* excel in minute description.

15. WILLIAM DEAN HOWELLS, the first of recent writers of prose, was born at Martinsville, Ohio, in 1837. He was a country editor until 1860, when he wrote a campaign life of Abraham Lincoln, which had a great circulation during that year. It was never acknowledged by the author, though as literature it was quite as good as Hawthorne's life of Pierce. In 1861 Mr. Howells was given the politically unimportant consulate at Venice. Never did an author make better literary use of his position, at the same time performing its official duties faithfully. Not until his return, in 1865, did he begin to publish the fruits of his Italian sight-seeings. *Venetian Life* appeared in 1866, and *Italian Journeys* the next year. Their descriptions were faultless, and their literary style of surprising excellence. After a brief period of editorship in New York, Mr. Howells went to Boston as assistant editor of *The Atlantic Monthly*, the controlling editorship of which he assumed on the retirement of Mr. James T. Fields, in 1871. *Suburban Sketches* (1871) did for Cambridge what *Venetian Life* had done for Venice, though its descriptions of the university town were less direct, and included many pieces of delicate humor and not a few delightful character-sketches. Every one of Mr. Howells's books, thus far, had increased his public of readers; but *Their*

Wedding Journey (1872) multiplied them anew, and showed him to be, by humor and descriptive power, the best literary painter of contemporary American life in the better classes. *A Chance Acquaintance* and *A Foregone Conclusion*, two other novels, were equally successful in the same vein. Mr. Howells's latest books have been a farce and two comedies: *The Parlor Car, Out of the Question*, and *A Counterfeit Presentment*. As a dramatist Mr. Howells is easily successful, for even in his stories the reader notes an abundance of dramatic situations, not the less telling because they are so often delicate. In 1860 a volume called *Poems of Two Friends* was written by Mr. Howells in conjunction with J. J. Piatt. His collected poems were afterwards issued in a single small volume. Many of them have become favorites, and their excellence of versification, especially in hexameters, is marked. Mr. Howells's unacknowledged work as editor is easily detected, such is the quality of his style.

16. THEODORE WINTHROP, a native of Connecticut and a graduate of Yale College, was killed in the first set engagement of the war, at Big Bethel, Virginia, on June 10, 1861. He had written a few spirited magazine sketches, and at his death three complete novels and a number of minor papers were found among his manuscripts. The novels, *Cecil Dreeme, John Brent,* and *Edwin Brothertoft,*

are the breeziest and heartiest of American works of fiction, and even their horses breathe a vital oxygen. The lesser sketches fill two volumes, mostly devoted to out-door papers of camp-life and travel.

17. EDWARD EGGLESTON, born in Indiana in 1837, has found a special field in novels of pioneer life in the uncivilized outposts of western civilization. His first mature years were those of a Methodist itinerant and Sunday-school worker. One or two books for children have since been found excellent, but his first general recognition as one of the most vigorous of American novelists followed the publication of *The Hoosier Schoolmaster* in 1871. *The End of the World*, *The Mystery of Metropolisville*, and *The Circuit Rider*, later stories, have similarly described to the letter the rough backwoods life of the hardy settlers of fifty years ago. These novels have been very popular in Europe, their vividness of description and unfamiliarity of subject being no less surprising to German readers than were Fenimore Cooper's Indian tales at the time of their first appearance.

18. JULIAN HAWTHORNE, a son of Nathaniel Hawthorne, born in Boston in 1846, has found his advancement hindered rather than aided by the circumstance of his birth, for he has inherited, to a large extent, his father's tastes and methods, so that his books have challenged comparison with

the works of the greatest of modern romancers. This comparison their own unquestionable excellence has enabled them to endure without essential damage. His novels are three, *Bressant* (1873), *Idolatry* (1874), and *Garth* (1877), weird studies of abnormal life, elaborated with much literary skill. Mr. Hawthorne has resided abroad of late years, and his sketches of German and English life and character have been uncommonly accurate, though their truthfulness of description have made some of them seem the work of a pitiless observer. These *Saxon Studies* and *English Studies* are worthy continuations of the elder Hawthorne's *Our Old Home*.

19. HENRY JAMES, JR., resembles Julian Hawthorne in literary painstaking, but his stories and sketches are less romantic and even more artistic. Mr. James describes men's ways and words, and leaves the reader to infer their character therefrom. *A Passionate Pilgrim* contains the best of the magazine stories he has written during the past twelve years. *Roderick Hudson*, *The American*, and *Watch and Ward* are as faultless as statues, but as cold. Mr. James has for some time lived in London. His *Transatlantic Sketches* consist of the best of his contributions from abroad to American magazines and newspapers.

20. ELIZABETH STUART PHELPS, a daughter of Professor Austin Phelps of the theological semi-

nary at Andover, is another of the writers of the remarkable short stories which distinguish the present time. The chief of her lesser tales are collected in *Men, Women, and Ghosts* (1869). Besides many Sunday-school stories, Miss Phelps has written three novels, *Hedged In* (1870), *The Silent Partner* (1871), and *The Story of Avis* (1877). The latter is her chief work, being a dramatic and highly-wrought record of the struggles of a woman's soul. Miss Phelps's somewhat infrequent poems are collected in a volume called *Poetic Studies. The Gates Ajar*, an original book on heaven, made a great literary sensation in 1868.

21. LOUISA MAY ALCOTT, a daughter of A. B. Alcott, is the best of American writers of juveniles. *Little Women* (1867) attained quick popularity. Its success in describing child-life lay in its entire freedom from artificiality and its cheeriness of spirit. Miss Alcott's literary style is wholly natural, but it is so free from blemishes that the reader never notices it at all. The bright New England boy and girl Miss Alcott knows very well, and her light humor and fertility of invention have made her other books for the young (seven in number) equal favorites. Their merit is nearly uniform, and their readers are of all ages. Miss Alcott's considerable novel of *Work* and her stories and sketches of adult life promise an elaborate work of fiction in the future.

22. HARRIET PRESCOTT SPOFFORD (born Harriet Elizabeth Prescott) is notable for the splendor of her style and the almost unhealthy luxuriance of her fancy. *Sir Rohan's Ghost* (1859), *The Amber Gods* (1863), *Azarian* (1864), *The Thief in the Night*, and *New England Legends* are her stories published in book form, though they represent but a small part of her printed writings. As the best example of her great powers of construction and elaboration may be mentioned the story of *Midsummer and May*, in the *Amber Gods* volume. Mrs. Spofford has never collected her poems.

23. OTHER NOVELISTS. — William M. Baker, long a Presbyterian minister in the Southwestern States, has illustrated its peculiarities and its people in *Inside, Mose Evans, The New Timothy*, and *Carter Quarterman*, eccentric novels in which the personal descriptions are better than the plots. Frank Lee Benedict is the author of six rapidly-moving stories in which middle-class American society receives an attractive presentation. J. W. De Forest has taken subjects for fiction from the same class in society, and an element of satire runs through his books. Hjalmar Hjorth Boyesen, a young Norwegian who has resided in this country but a few years, has written in English clear and beautiful stories of his native land, of which *Gunnar, a Norse Romance* is the chief. In fiction, as in poetry, the number of recent female authors of merit is large. Mrs. Re-

becca Harding Davis, the author of *Margret Howth* and *Waiting for the Verdict*, has great power in the delineation of the sad and solemn sides of life, especially in the lower classes. Mrs. Richard S. Greenough's stories have a sombre hue and an artistic finish. Mrs. Adeline D. T. Whitney's *Leslie Goldthwaite* is a lovely picture of young girlhood, which the author has illustrated in several other stories. Mrs. Louise Chandler Moulton's *Some Women's Hearts* is a collection of novelettes having grace and power. *One Summer*, by Blanche Willis Howard, is the most agreeable of recent love-stories, and a somewhat remarkable instance of a praiseworthy first book. It appeared in 1875, and was followed in 1877 by a collection of European sketches by the same author. Mrs. Frances Hodgson Burnett, after publishing many short stories in the magazines, produced in 1877 *That Lass o' Lowrie's*, a novel of life in the Lancashire mines of England, having great power of plot and description, and remarkable for its mastery of the dialect and customs of an unfamiliar region. Three novels by the late Mrs. Anne M. Crane Seemuller, of Baltimore, deserve mention for their morbid strength: *Emily Chester*, *Opportunity*, and *Reginald Archer*.

24. AMERICAN HUMOR. — There has never been any lack of humor in American literature, from the time of Richard Alsop and the Hartford wits down to the latest newspaper paragraph. It has been

individual rather than general and its rapidity of thought is its chief characteristic. Our lack of a literary centre has denied us any *Punch* or *Kladderadatsch*, but as a compensation every country paper keeps its own clown. A really witty saying goes from Eastport to San Francisco, and thus a Seba Smith ("Major Jack Downing"), B. P. Shillaber ("Mrs. Partington"), or George D. Prentice is likely to find his public greater than his reputation, and his reputation more generous than his purse. Our later humorists have won their celebrity by the constant publication of longer sketches, good, bad, or indifferent, being only careful that the name go with the sketch, and that the sketch be individual enough and long enough to keep out of the promiscuous limbo of popular quotation. George H. Derby ("John Phœnix") was born in Massachusetts in 1823, and graduated at West Point in 1846. His wit was genuine and all his own, and his California sketches made delightful fun of that region in the gold-mining excitement of 1849. Perhaps his cleverest achievement was his issue of an illustrated journal, in which the familiar little advertising cuts of the daily papers were made to do duty in all sorts of odd fashions. Charles Farrar Browne ("Artemus Ward") was born at Waterford, Maine, in 1834. His humor was of an uneven quality, and was often coarse; but toward the last of his life he so ripened and mellowed that his popular nickname of "Artemus the delicious" was not wholly inappropriate. He first popularized misspelling in America, and in view of this fact we may call his best saying the remark that "Chaucer was a great poet, but he could n't spell." Browne won much success as a lecturer, and died in England in 1867, having made himself a great favorite in London, where he served for some time on the staff of *Punch*. Henry W. Shaw ("Josh Billings"), born in Massachusetts in 1818, is chiefly known as the writer of proverbs and aphorisms, in which wit and wisdom are neatly combined. They are, like Artemus Ward's sayings, in phonetic spelling, but gain nothing by their presentation in uncouth form. David Ross Locke was born in Vestal, Broome County, New York, in 1833, and in his early years led a varied life as a country printer and editor. In 1860 he began the publication of letters by "Petroleum V. Nasby," an entirely original character, whose epistles became famous during the war, and exerted a very considerable political influence. Locke is the chief political satirist of the time, and Nasby, whether pastor, reformer, workingman, or member of society, is a constant caricature of the ideas for which he stands. Unlike other national satirical humorists taking public affairs for their theme, Locke is facile in turning to the most recent questions with unabated strength and undimmed humor. Another humorist, writing during the war upon political themes, but choosing subjects of a more local character, and having a less definite purpose in his satire, was Robert H. Newell ("Orpheus C. Kerr"), a native of New York city. Samuel Langhorne Clemens ("Mark Twain"), like so many other humorists, first attracted attention in California. *The Innocents Abroad*, a burlesque history of the absurd doings of a somewhat whimsical expedition which had really visited the Mediterranean countries, won thousands of readers, and *Roughing It* and *The Gilded Age* (with Charles Dudley Warner) were not less successful. The qualities of Mr. Clemens's style are peculiar, slyness and adroitness in jesting being prominent, so that the reader is treated to a constant succession of surprises.

25. CHARLES DUDLEY WARNER is a humorist of a more delicate type than those just mentioned. He was born in Plainfield, Massachusetts, in 1829, and graduated at Hamilton College, in 1851. *My Summer in a Garden*, a series of delightful sketches of amateur horticulture, first made him famous. *Backlog Studies*, domestic and moral reflections, was less popular, but equally successful. *Baddeck, and That Sort of Thing* followed, being an account of a trip to the provinces of British North America. Its little bits of fun and humor are scattered all through the book, and are to be enjoyed in exact proportion to the reader's own tastes. *Mum-*

mies and Moslems, *In the Levant*, and *Saunterings* similarly, though a little more soberly, illuminate life in Oriental and European countries visited by the author. In *Being a Boy* (1877) Mr. Warner draws the New England youngster to the life.

26. JAMES PARTON, a native of England but long a resident of New York, has devoted the greater part of his literary life to the production of biographies of prominent men, written after a careful collation of authorities, but addressed to the popular taste in their fluent style and attractive allusion. Aaron Burr, Andrew Jackson, Benjamin Franklin, Thomas Jefferson, General Butler, and Horace Greeley have thus been described in volumes of considerable size, while a single volume has been compiled from similar biographical sketches of less length. Mr. Parton has also edited serviceable collections of humorous poetry and French lyrics, and has prepared a general history of caricature and caricaturists, besides collecting elaborate materials for a life of Voltaire.

27. EDWARD E. HALE, born in Boston in 1822, of a family well known in the literary history of that city, has written a large number of very readable and ingenious stories, of which *Ten Times One is Ten* is the longest, a tale made famous by the cheery motto of its hero, Harry Wadsworth. Mr. Hale's short sketch of *A Man without a Country* is the most remarkable piece of verisimilitude

produced on this side the water. It exerted a marked influence in strengthening the Northern arms during the war. In *Philip Nolan's Friends* Mr. Hale has written a continuous novel of some length, marked by his usual cleverness of plot and phrase.

28. THOMAS WENTWORTH HIGGINSON, a descendant of one of the most ancient of Massachusetts families, and a Harvard graduate of 1841, is an essayist pure and simple, and is an especially delightful companion in his *Out-Door Papers* (1863) and *Oldport Days* (1873), volumes made up chiefly of articles concerning this or that phase of out-door life. In *Atlantic Essays* (1871) there is a greater proportion of papers on classical or literary subjects. Colonel Higginson was at the head of a colored regiment between 1862 and 1864, having been all his life an active opponent of slavery. *Army Life in a Black Regiment* (1870) details his South Carolina experiences. In his *Young Folks' History of the United States* (1875) he presents, within small compass, a readable and impartial story of the growth of the country. *Malbone* (1869), a romance of Newport life, is his only novel.

29. MISCELLANEOUS WRITERS. — Six authors remain to be mentioned, who cannot conveniently be classed under any special head. Edmund Quincy, who was born in 1808 and died in 1877, was a constant contributor of unsigned articles to

the periodical press, and wrote a forgotten but meritorious novel, *Wensley*, in 1853. He will longest be remembered, however, as the author of a life of his father, President Josiah Quincy, of Harvard. This biography is a thoroughly charming history of a man whom James Russell Lowell properly calls "a great public character." James T. Fields, of Boston, whose poems have been previously mentioned, has enjoyed the acquaintance of more English and American authors than any other of our writers, and he has preserved some of his entertaining reminiscences in *Yesterdays with Authors*. In *Underbrush* (1877) are contained his lighter essays and sketches. Mary Abigail Dodge ("Gail Hamilton") is the author of many volumes of bright essays on a great variety of current topics, and of *First Love is Best*, a commendable novel of modern life. Thomas Starr King, a Unitarian minister in Boston and San Francisco, left at his death, in 1864, no considerable book save a very accurate and serviceable account of *The White Hills*, of which he was an enthusiastic admirer. He was a favorite lecturer, and his eloquence did much to prevent the agitation of secession in California. In 1867 selections from his sermons and lectures appeared under the titles of *Christianity and Humanity* and *Substance and Show*. John Fiske, the son of a brilliant *littérateur* of Hartford, graduated at Harvard in 1864 and immediately won reputation as a student of modern philosophy. In his *Outlines of Cosmic Philosophy* is presented a better exposition of the Spencerian system than one gets from a casual reading of Herbert Spencer himself. *Myths and Myth-Makers* is a volume in which folk-lore is explained according to modern scientific principles. In *The Unseen World, and other Essays* are literary reviews and able musical criticisms. Mr. Fiske has also written a clever *brochure* in defense of the moderate use of tobacco and alcohol, in opposition to a magazine attack thereon by James Parton. Joseph Cook, like Mr. Fiske well acquainted with the latest scientific literature, expounds directly opposite theological and philosophical opinions, and brings to the defense of evangelical doctrines a logical method and an uncommon rhetorical skill.

INDEX.

Abbot, Ezra, 37.
Abbott, Jacob, 71.
Abbott, John Sebastian Cabot, 71.
Adams, Hannah, 28.
Adams, John, 23.
Adams, Nehemiah, 31.
Agassiz, Louis, 84.
Alcott, Amos Bronson, 81.
Alcott, Louisa May, 102.
Aldrich, Thomas Bailey, 93.
Alexander, Archibald, 31.
Alexander, James Waddell, 31.
Alexander, Joseph, 31.
Alger, William Rounseville, 36.
Allen, Elizabeth Akers, 97.
Allston, Washington, 47.
Audubon, John James, 84.
Bacon, Delia, 83.
Baker, William Mumford, 103.
Bancroft, George, 67.
Bancroft, Hubert Howard, 84.
Barlow, Joel, 27.
Barnes, Albert, 37.
Bartol, Cyrus Augustus, 32.
Barton, Benjamin Smith, 29.
Beecher, Henry Ward, 37.
Beecher, Lyman, 31.
Belknap, Jeremy, 28.
Bellows, Henry Whitney, 32.
Benedict, Frank Lee, 103.
Bird, Robert Montgomery, 77.
Boker, George Henry, 64.

Bowditch, Nathaniel, 84.
Boyesen, Hjalmar Hjorth, 103.
Bradstreet, Anne, 15.
Brainard, John Gardiner Calkins, 47.
Brainerd, David, 21.
Brewer, Thomas Mayo, 84.
Briggs, Charles Frederick, 78.
Brooks, Charles Timothy, 65.
Brooks, Phillips, 37.
Brown, Charles Brockden, 28.
Browne, Charles Farrar, 105.
Browne, John Ross, 71.
Brownell, Henry Howard, 96.
Bryant, William Cullen, 48.
Burnett, Frances Hodgson, 104.
Bush, George, 36.
Bushnell, Horace, 37.
Butler, William Allen, 66.
Calhoun, John Caldwell, 66.
Calvert, George Henry, 64.
Carleton, William M., 93.
Carey, Henry Charles, 84.
Cary, Alice, 66.
Cary, Phœbe, 66.
Channing, William Ellery, 32.
Channing, William Ellery, Jr., 81.
Child, Francis James, 84.
Child, Lydia Maria, 82.
Choate, Rufus, 66.
Clarke, James Freeman, 32.
Clay, Henry, 66.
Clemens, Samuel Langhorne, 107.

Conant, Thomas J., 36.
Conway, Moncure Daniel, 32.
Cook, Joseph, 111.
Cooke, John Esten, 78.
Cooke, Rose Terry, 97.
Cooper, James Fenimore, 72.
Coues, Elliott, 84.
Cozzens, Frederick Swartwout, 83.
Cranch, Christopher Pearse, 65.
Cummins, Maria S., 79.
Curtis, George William, 81.
Cutler, Elbridge Jefferson, 96.
Dana, James Dwight, 84.
Dana, Richard Henry, 46.
Dana, Richard Henry, Jr., 82.
Davis, Rebecca Harding, 104.
De Forest, John William, 103.
Derby, George H., 105.
Dewey, Orville, 31.
Dexter, Henry Martyn, 36.
Dodge, Mary Abigail, 110.
Drake, Joseph Rodman, 44.
Draper, John William, 86.
Dwight, Timothy, 18.
Edwards, Jonathan, 16.
Eggleston, Edward, 100.
Eliot, John, 12.
Eliot, Samuel, 71.
Emerson, Ralph Waldo, 80
Emmons, Nathaniel, 18.
English, Thomas Dunn, 64.
Everett, Edward, 66.
Fawcett, Edgar, 92.
Fields, James Thomas, 110.
Finney, Charles G., 37.
Fiske, John, 110.
Folger, Peter, 15.
Franklin, Benjamin, 18.
Freneau, Philip, 27.
Frothingham, Octavius Brooks, 32.
Frothingham, Richard, 70.
Furness, Horace Howard, 83.

Furness, William Henry, 31.
Garrison, William Lloyd, 66.
Gilder, Richard Watson, 97.
Gillett, Edward H., 36.
Godwin, Parke, 71.
Goodrich, Samuel Griswold, 83.
Gray, Asa, 84.
Greeley, Horace, 86.
Greene, Albert Gorton, 47.
Greene, George Washington, 71.
Greenough, Mrs. R. S., 104.
Guyot, Arnold, 84.
Hadley, James, 84.
Haldeman, Samuel Stehman, 84.
Hale, Edward Everett, 108.
Hall, Charles Francis, 71.
Hall, John, 37.
Halleck, Fitz-Greene, 45.
Halleck, Henry Wager, 84.
Halpine, Charles Graham, 93.
Hamilton, Alexander, 25.
Hardee, William J., 84.
Harris, Miriam Coles, 79.
Harte, Francis Bret, 92.
Hawthorne, Julian, 100.
Hawthorne, Nathaniel, 74.
Hay, John, 92.
Hayes, Isaac Israel, 71.
Hayne, Paul Hamilton, 96.
Henry, Patrick, 23.
Herbert, Henry William, 83.
Hickok, Laurens Perseus, 35.
Higginson, Thomas Wentworth, 109.
Hildreth, Richard, 67.
Hillard, George Stillman, 82.
Hillhouse, James Abraham, 47.
Hitchcock, Edward, 84.
Hodge, Charles, 34.
Hoffman, Charles Fenno, 64.
Holland, Josiah Gilbert, 83.
Holmes, Abiel, 29.
Holmes, Nathaniel, 83.

INDEX.

Holmes, Oliver Wendell, 58.
Hooker, Thomas, 10.
Hopkins, Mark, 35.
Hopkins, Samuel, 18.
Hopkinson, Francis, 29.
Howard, Blanche Willis, 104.
Howe, Julia Ward, 96.
Howells, William Dean, 98.
Hughes, John, 37.
Irving, Peter, 40.
Irving, Washington, 38.
Irving, William, 39.
Jackson, Helen Fiske, 97.
James, Henry, 36.
James, Henry, Jr., 101.
Jay, John, 25.
Jefferson, Thomas, 24.
Jones, Charles Colcock, 84.
Judd, Sylvester, 78.
Kane, Elisha Kent, 71.
Kennedy, John Pendleton, 79.
Kent, James, 84.
Key, Francis Scott, 47.
Kimball, Richard Burleigh, 78.
King, Thomas Starr, 110.
Kirk, John Foster, 70.
Knox, Thomas W., 71.
Lanier, Sidney, 97.
Larcom, Lucy, 97.
Lathrop, George Parsons, 97.
Ledyard, John, 29.
Leland, Charles Godfrey, 93.
Lewis, Tayler, 36.
Lippincott, Sara Jane, 79.
Livingston, William, 22.
Locke, David Ross, 106.
Longfellow, Henry Wadsworth, 50.
Loomis, Elias, 84.
Lossing, Benson John, 71.
Lowell, James Russell, 60.
Madison, James, 25.
March, Francis Andrew, 84.

Marsh, George Perkins, 84.
Marsh, James, 35.
Marshall, John, 29.
Mather, Cotton, 10.
Mather, Increase, 10.
Mayo, William Starbuck, 78.
McClellan, George Brinton, 84.
McClintock, John, 37.
McClurg, James, 28.
McCosh, James, 34.
Melville, Herman, 79.
Menken, Adah Isaacs, 92.
Miller, Joaquin, 91.
Mitchell, Donald Grant, 83.
Mitchill, Samuel Latham, 29.
Morris, George P., 64.
Motley, John Lothrop, 69.
Moulton, Louise Chandler, 104.
Muhlenberg, William Augustus, 47.
Neal, John, 78.
Neal, Joseph Clay, 82.
Newcomb, Simon, 84.
Newell, Robert Henry, 107.
Nordhoff, Charles, 82.
Norton, Andrews, 31.
Norton, Charles Eliot, 82.
Olmsted, Frederick Law, 71.
Otis, James, 23.
Paine, Robert Treat, Jr., 27.
Paine, Thomas, 26.
Palfrey, John Gorham, 68.
Park, Edwards Amasa, 31.
Parker, Theodore, 32.
Parkman, Francis, 70.
Parsons, Theophilus, 36.
Parsons, Thomas William, 65.
Parton, James, 108.
Parton, Sarah Willis, 79.
Paulding, James Kirke, 43.
Payne, John Howard, 47.
Peabody, Andrew Preston, 32.
Peirce, Benjamin, 84.

Percival, James Gates, 64.
Perry, Nora, 97.
Perry, William Stevens, 36.
Phelps, Elizabeth Stuart, 101.
Phillips, Wendell, 66.
Piatt, John James, 95.
Piatt, Sarah Morgan Bryan, 95.
Pinkney, Edward Coate, 64.
Poe, Edgar Allan, 63.
Porter, Noah, 35.
Prescott, William Hickling, 69.
Preston, Margaret Junkin, 97.
Punchard, George, 36.
Quincy, Edmund, 109.
Quincy, Josiah, Jr., 23.
Ramsay, David, 28.
Read, Thomas Buchanan, 96.
Reed, Henry, 83.
Reed, William Bradford, 83.
Robinson, Edward, 83.
Rumford, Count, 29.
Rush, Benjamin, 29.
Sands, Robert Charles, 49.
Sandys, George, 9.
Saxe, John Godfrey, 89.
Schaff, Philip, 36.
Schoolcraft, Henry Rowe, 84.
Schuyler, Eugene, 71.
Scott, Winfield, 87.
Sedgwick, Catherine Maria, 79.
Seemuller, Anne Crane, 104.
Seward, William Henry, 66.
Shaw, Henry W., 106.
Shedd, William Greenough Thayer, 36.
Sherman, William Tecumseh, 87.
Simms, William Gilmore, 78.
Smith, John, 14.
Sophocles, Evangelinus Apostolides, 84.
Spalding, Martin John, 37.
Sparks, Jared, 70.

Spofford, Harriet Prescott, 103.
Sprague, Charles, 47.
Squier, Ephraim George, 71.
Stedman, Edmund Clarence, 95.
Stephens, Alexander Hamilton, 86.
Stephens, John Lloyd, 71.
Stevens, Abel, 36.
Stith, William, 21.
Stoddard, Richard Henry, 89.
Story, William Wetmore, 65.
Stowe, Harriet Beecher, 79.
Street, Alfred Billings, 49.
Stuart, Moses, 31.
Sumner, Charles, 66.
Taylor, Bayard, 88.
Taylor, Nathaniel William, 37.
Taylor, William Mackergo, 37.
Thaxter, Celia, 97.
Thoreau, Henry David, 81.
Ticknor, George, 81.
Timrod, Henry, 96.
Todd, John, 31.
Torrey, John, 84.
Trowbridge, John Townsend, 90.
Trumbull, John, 27.
Tuckerman, Henry Theodore, 83.
Upham, Thomas Cogswell, 35.
Verplanck, Gulian Crommelin, 49.
Ward, Nathaniel, 14.
Ware, Henry, 31.
Ware, Henry, Jr., 31.
Ware, William, 78.
Warner, Anna, 79.
Warner, Charles Dudley, 107.
Warner, Susan, 79.
Washington, George, 24.
Wayland, Francis, 36.
Webster, Daniel, 66.
Webster, Noah, 84.
Wheatley, Phillis, 27.
Wheaton, Henry, 84.
Whipple, Edwin Percy, 82.

INDEX.

White, Richard Grant, 83.
Whitman, Walt, 90.
Whitney, Adeline D. Train, 104.
Whitney, William Dwight, 84.
Whittier, John Greenleaf, 56.
Wigglesworth, Michael, 15.
Wilde, Richard Henry, 47.
Wilkes, Charles, 71.
Williams, Roger, 13.
Willis, Nathaniel Parker, 64.
Willson, Forceythe, 96.
Wilson, Alexander, 29.

Wilson, Henry, 86.
Winter, William, 97.
Winthrop, John, 14.
Winthrop, Robert Charles, 66.
Winthrop, Theodore, 99.
Wirt, William, 29.
Woods, Leonard, 31.
Woodworth, Samuel, 47.
Woolman, John, 21.
Woolsey, Theodore Dwight, 84.
Worcester, Joseph Emerson, 84.
Worcester, Noah, 31.